ABC

THE
ALPHABETICAL
ENTREPRENEUR

26 Character Traits for Startup Success

GREGORY SMITH
ILLUSTRATIONS BY JESSICA NEWTON

Black Lake Press
TELL YOUR STORY

BLACKLAKEPRESS.COM

Illustrations and cover design by Jessica Newton
Editorial by Cory Lakatos
Published by Black Lake Press of
Holland, Michigan

Black Lake Press is a division of
Black Lake Studio, LLC
Direct inquiries to Black Lake Press at
www.blacklakepress.com
ISBN-13: 978-0-9913095-0-4

To the entrepreneurs of downtown Holland, Michigan.
You have made it a special place to live and do business.
Thank you.

ACKNOWLEDGEMENTS

A book is a product of many hands, seen and unseen. As always, there are lots of people who deserve thanks but not enough space to thank everyone who made this happen, directly or indirectly. Here are a few that most deserve mention.

To my wife and children. You loved me enough to let me learn the lessons in this book as I was building my own business, and paid the tuition for my entrepreneurial education. Thank you.

To Jessica Newton, my illustrator at Black Lake. You gave the book a whimsical look, and your fun images take the edge off some of the hard words. I'll be forever grateful for your inspired cover design.

To Cory Lakatos, my ever-efficient, ever-effective, and ever-enduring editor and publishing assistant. You continue to keep me from looking stupid in print. What more could I ask?

To my entrepreneurial colleagues and clients. I've been watching you and taking notes for years. Your ups, downs, and questions gave me my material.

Finally, to all of my lefty professors who criticized and demeaned entrepreneurs every chance they got: *no soup for you!*

ACKNOWLEDGEMENTS

INTRODUCTION

Almost everyone I meet has three things in common:

1. They have a great idea for a movie.
2. They're going to write a book. Someday.
3. They want to own their own business. That way, they could control their own destiny and be their own boss.

I get it, I really do. I'm a big believer in daydreams; if nothing else, they entertain you and keep your spirits up when life is dull or difficult. But let's do a reality check on those three particular dreams.

First, however great your movie idea is, it's not original. Thousands of movie ideas float around Hollywood every year. Hollywood isn't looking for new ideas, it's looking for well-done, finished scripts and the confidence that producing one of them will provide a reasonable return on investment. So, don't tell me your idea. Go write a great script and organize financing.

Second, I've written over two-dozen books. Want to know the trick? One sentence at a time. I figured out that the average novel has something like six thousand sentences. Get busy.

Third, there's nothing stopping you from starting a business except you—but you're a big hurdle. Whether it happens, or whether it succeeds, largely depends on you. That's what this book is about.

One of the most sacred spots in ancient Greece was the temple at Delphi. Inside was a priestess called the Pythia, who was the voice of the god Apollo. People would travel to Delphi, make an offering, and be allowed to go inside to ask a question about their future. The Pythia would consult Apollo and give a cryptic answer. Engraved over the entrance to the oracle's chamber were two words. They were advice, admonition, and advance warning: "Know Thyself."

The oracle may have been nothing more than an upscale fortune-teller, but those two words stand the test of time. We cannot unravel the threads of our future unless and until we solve the puzzle of our own identity. Otherwise, our future is nothing but vague shadows and possibilities. Who we really are deep down inside determines whether and when and how those shadows will take shape and become solid.

OK, enough about the Greeks. Let's talk about that business you would love to own.

Some potential entrepreneurs do all sorts of research and preparation. They go to workshops and conferences. They surf the web and talk to other business owners. They buy (and occasionally even read parts of) books. They investigate their product and market. They learn how to use business software. And some put enormous effort into getting their name and logo just right, fretting over what title to give themselves on their business cards. The brand and logo and title are the incarnation of their daydream, a projection of their idealized inner self—an inner self many of them don't really know.

Too many wannabe entrepreneurs don't spend enough time asking themselves if they're really cut out for this. Are they the kind of people, or are they capable of growing into the kind of people, who can survive owning their own company? Set aside success—you have to survive before you can succeed. Would you even survive? Do you know yourself well enough to answer that question?

Most of the skills you need can be learned or hired. You can buy tools and contract people to balance your books and build your website. But what really determines your survival? Your temperament and personality. Deeper than that, your *character*. Do you have enough imagination, judgment, self-discipline, and self-awareness? Can you solve problems and make payroll when everything feels uphill and against the wind? Do you have the passion to care but the emotional detachment to make hard decisions, even if it means firing your best friend? None of these can be delegated or subcontracted, and they certainly can't be ignored. If you don't have them, it will become very obvious, probably very soon.

You may have demonstrated some of these traits in your career while working for someone else, but that doesn't guarantee that you have them in the right tone or measure to be in the top slot. You might have been a great employee precisely because you were free of ultimate responsibility—it gave you a measure of freedom to think and act. That responsibility can be paralyzing; I've seen former corporate vice presidents who can't run their own coffee shop. Things get really real, really fast when there's no one to back you up.

So, do you know yourself well enough to start that business you've been dreaming about? Are you cut out for this? I hope this book helps you figure that out, because starting a successful business is not a function of just wanting it badly enough. Motivational speakers build their own businesses convincing people that motivation is all that matters for entrepreneurial success. These gurus point to their own success as evidence—but they're selling motivational books. Now, of course motivation matters, but it's obviously not all that matters. If it were, I'd spend my summers and falls quarterbacking the Denver Broncos and my winters in the south of France painting in the Expressionist style. When starting a business, motivation without talent and a lot of other qualities will only breed frustration and futility.

What are those other qualities? This book is an attempt to articulate twenty-six of them.

As you read, be honest with yourself. After all, who are you trying to fool? But don't be afraid, either: hundreds of millions—maybe billions—of men and women have been their own bosses. They've been butchers and bakers and candlestick makers the world over. Being an entrepreneur or small business owner isn't like being an astronaut, something that only a handful of folks can do. It's more like being a fireman, fisherman, or farmer: the requirements aren't rare, but they are particular. You either have them, or you don't. If you do, you'll do fine, but if you don't, it's going to be a tough slog.

In stressing how important he thought the motto of the Oracle of Delphi was, the philosopher Socrates said, "The unexamined life is not worth living." For the entrepreneur, the unexamined life will be a beast that bites you over and over again. If you've already started a business, use this book to take a fearless inventory and make a plan to grow into what you've begun. If you're still deciding whether to launch yourself into the entrepreneurial life, let's see if you've got what it takes.

A IS FOR ADAPTABLE

You probably don't remember Gumby.

Gumby was a claymation cartoon character in an early-1960s children's TV show. Gumby was a tall, lanky proto-hipster made of green clay. His legs flared so he looked like he was wearing bell-bottom pants and he got around by sliding on one foot like he was riding a skateboard. He had a sidekick: a talking orange pony (this *was* the 60s). And because he was made of clay, he could bend and smoosh into any shape. When I was little, I (and millions of other kids) had a Gumby action figure. It was soft rubber with wire inside, and you could bend and flex Gumby any way your demented seven-year-old mind imagined.

Entrepreneurs are often told they should be flexible like Gumby, but that's terrible advice. Entrepreneurs aren't flexible like Gumby. Great entrepreneurs are *adaptable*. Not flexible, adaptable. There's a crucial difference.

Do you know what a riptide is? Sometimes a current forms at a beach, sucking everything from the waterline back out through the waves, away from the shore. If you're swimming or surfing, you can find yourself moving out to sea without warning at ten or twenty miles per hour. Flexible means going *with* the current. But surviving (much less succeeding) in a riptide does not mean going with the current. Nor does it mean pointlessly swimming against it and exhausting yourself until hypothermia sets in and you drown. To survive a riptide, you must *escape* it. That means changing the game and doing something counterintuitive: swimming perpendicular to it. Most riptides are, at most, only a few hundred yards wide. They're basically rivers running out to sea. The trick to escaping is to swim parallel to the shore, at a right angle to the current. With effort, you can get out.

Gumby—good old flexible, charming, likable Gumby—goes

A is for
ADAPTABLE

with the flow. He's so cool that he lets the current carry him out to where he gets eaten by a claymation shark.

Successful entrepreneurs change the game, change tactics, change themselves, make a counterintuitive move, find another direction at a right angle to where everyone else is being carried—and then swim like hell until they succeed. Or they drown trying. No, entrepreneurs aren't flexible like Gumby. They're adaptable—like a cockroach.

Consider the humble, disrespected cockroach. After the nuclear war or the asteroid strike or the zombie apocalypse, you know what will crawl out of the rubble and start selling the survivors stuff? Cockroaches and entrepreneurs.

Back in 1999, there was mass hysteria around the supposed "Y2K problem." The idea was that none of the computers were programed to turn their internal clocks over to the year 2000 (don't ask—nothing happened at midnight). But I remember friends going to warehouse stores and buying pallets of toilet paper to stash in their basements. Why? Yeah, that's what I wondered, so I asked. They told me that when the computers stopped at the turn of the millennium, the cash registers wouldn't work and the stores wouldn't be able to sell us things. I remember replying, "Look, even if the register doesn't work, someone will find a way to sell you toilet paper. Trust me: if there are people who want to buy, someone will get out a pencil, add up sums, and start taking cash or trade." The entrepreneurs, the indestructible cockroaches of any economy, will still be standing and selling toilet paper or whatever the marketplace demands.

Flexibility means going with the market. Adaptability means finding new markets when existing markets change or shrink. Adaptable entrepreneurs discover new products and services to meet demand. They invent new ways to deliver them to buyers. They don't bend in the wind or go with the flow; they work like hell to not get blown over, escape the current, move the river. They make it work—no, more that that, they find a way to win, whatever happens. Cockroaches adapt. They survive when the ecosystem shifts. They create new opportunities when doors close. They reinvent themselves. They succeed where merely flexible personalities fizzle and fail.

There's an old cliché about an army planning for battle: plans last until the first bullet is fired; after that, you're adapting to the fog of war. The one that adapts most quickly, most shrewdly, wins. In fact, United States Marines are not taught to be flexible in a crisis. They are taught to: "Improvise. Adapt. Overcome."

When markets change, entrepreneurs, like Marines, improvise, adapt, and overcome. They reimagine, retool, and reorient. They evolve. The tree that bends in the wind isn't a good metaphor for an entrepreneur because long before the tree bent, it adapted to a windy environment. It's only capable of change within a very narrow range ("get bendy when it gets windy"). But natural selection is a heartless bitch: if the climate gets hotter/colder, wetter/drier, or if the forest gets invaded by boll weevils or herds of hungry giraffes, the bending-in-the-wind trick won't save it. It will have to adapt, to evolve, to reinvent itself to merely survive, much less thrive, in new conditions.

It's always been this way: adaptable entrepreneurs make marketplaces work. In every country, in every language, in every century, they've found a way to sell something to someone. When a new empire blew into town, planted a flag, and brought a new set of demands and incentives, the entrepreneurs adapted. They switched products, found new suppliers, found new ways to finance. They sold fish or wool or spices or services or cell phones to the Babylonians, the Greeks, the Romans, the Franks, the Vikings, the British, the teeming millions of the emerging Indian or Chinese middle classes with money burning holes in their pockets. They came up with letters of credit, cash discounts, layaway programs, revolving credit, service plans—whatever it took. They are usually despised by writers, artists, and politicians, depicted as greedy, possessed of a reptilian cunning, and given to manipulative scheming. But the adaptable, entrepreneurial cockroaches of history made much of history possible. They supplied the food, the weapons, and the boots for armies, and allowed kings to finance their ambitions. They produced and sold the wine for weddings. They cut the timber, got it to market, and used it to build the ships that explored the oceans. They put the cargo into the ships that made the journeys worthwhile. They delivered the purple dyes, made from exotic seashells, that colored the royal robes. They were the merchants who traveled the Spice Road, making trades at every stop, enduring the tirades and turnover of princes, the rage of armies, the devastation of plagues. No matter what or where or when, entrepreneurs found a way to adapt, to produce and provide goods and services. To survive. To win.

Adaptability is a response to change. For all those entrepreneurs who did adapt when change came, history is littered with the carcasses of those who didn't, who were merely flexible and went with the current until they drowned—who bent until they broke.

Let Gumby bend to his heart's content. You? Be an entrepreneur. Be a cockroach. Adapt.

B is for
BRAVE

B IS FOR BRAVE

When I was coming up with a word that starts with B to describe entrepreneurs, I almost used one that commonly denotes manly courage and rhymes with part of the phrase "halls of justice." But your kids might read this, so let's just say that to be an entrepreneur, you'd better be *brave*.

When I was in high school, I crewed on a large racing sailboat in the Pacific Ocean. I loved the boat's name: *Temerity*. Temerity is confidence bordering on recklessness, an almost foolhardy contempt for danger or opposition. Genuine entrepreneurs are brave to the point of temerity.

If you won't take risks, you're not a real entrepreneur. If success was guaranteed and there was no chance of losing your investment, everyone would start a business. Sadly, there are always people who want the rewards of entrepreneurship without the risk. I've met plenty of them, and they come in three flavors.

The first type is the daydreamer. These people fantasize about being their own boss, the captain of their own destiny, calling the shots, seizing the bull by the horns, making big bucks while bossing others around without having to work like a slave. They've nursed this daydream for years, rolling it around in their head every time they've hated their job or watched others succeed. They've cooked up all sorts of imaginary scenarios for products, services, markets, etc. They almost always figure out what they would name the business before they figure out what it would make or sell. Most of them have never started anything before. They've been waiting until just the right moment, when they can be sure it's a sure thing. They talk and talk and talk a big game but they never jump into the pool and get wet, because when they get to the end of the diving board and stare down at the possibility of failure and personal loss, they chicken out. They back away from the edge, telling themselves that the timing and conditions just aren't yet right.

The second type is the formerly successful corporate executive. These folks are smart, skilled, and successful. The problem is that all of their success has come from being a cog in someone else's machine. They may have hired and fired a thousand people in their career, run departments and divisions, flown around the world twenty times in first class, launched brands, and won awards. But they were always gambling with the house's money. Their own capital wasn't at risk. Hiring meant picking from applicants, not accepting responsibility for making payroll out of their retirement account or their mortgage payment. They may have managed the office budget, but they didn't have to choose between paying the rent or their kid's college tuition, or between buying equipment or putting braces on their child's teeth. These folks are spellbinding when they talk about their business plan—some of them have been writing multimillion-dollar business plans for thirty years—but never for their *own* business. More times than I can count, I've seen them freeze when it's time to pull the trigger because at the last minute it occurs to them that they're risking their nest egg and they freak out. I've had these folks tell me that they won't put in even modest amounts of startup capital (sums that the average restaurant or shop owner doesn't even blink at anymore) unless they can be guaranteed success—a condition that any restaurant or shop owner would laugh at. They won't play unless they know they can win, so they don't play.

The first two types are understandable, given human nature. But the third type is unsavory on principle: **the "entrepreneur" who just wants to burn OPM (Other People's Money).** As long as there have been governments and gullible investors, these types have been around. They have big plans and make big promises, but it's never their own skin in the game. They talk people and institutions into funding their ventures. Sometimes they even run Ponzi schemes. But there's a sucker born every minute, and these pseudo-entrepreneurs are always ready to spend a sucker's cash.

I hear a lot of ideas for startups, but in the last few years I've noticed a disturbing trend: more and more of them have business models that will *never* make money but are premised on getting government grants. For example, in the last ten years I've heard lots of pitches for green energy businesses that *can't* be profitable without public subsidies. When you point out that they're going to lose money every single day they operate, the "entrepreneur" looks you in the eye and tells you that it doesn't matter. I remember being at a startup competition and hearing a young man pitch his idea for a bicycle-sharing program in a downtown area. There would be coin-operated racks on every corner, and for a nominal fee the public could check bikes out to pedal around the metro area. I was on the panel of judges, and I asked him whether he had calculated the percentage of bikes that would end up broken, stolen, or left in the wrong places and have to be moved back into position every evening. He wasn't sure. Then I asked how he would calculate the rental fee. Was he sure that it would be enough to cover his losses? He wasn't sure. I asked how, with this uncertainty, he expected to get funded for the startup, including his salary as the executive director of the program. His answer: it didn't matter, because once started the program would operate on federal grants that made up for losses.

If you don't have skin in the game, you'll never make good business decisions. You won't *have* to. You'll never learn the thousand little lessons that everyone who's ever owned so much as a hotdog cart has had to learn. Entrepreneurs must be willing to hold the line, to stand in an empty shop and watch the mailman pass by, not delivering the customer check they need to keep the doors open. They must count down the days until the next payroll is due. They have to be willing to order supplies before they have orders to fill. They need courage to drive home at night knowing their house is mortgaged to the max and that they've borrowed all the money they can from parents and extended family. Entrepreneurship, the real thing, is about risk because if you own the possibility of winning you also have to own the possibility of losing. That's the real world.

And that takes courage, real courage. The courage that anyone who's ever been brave enough to start a flower shop had to learn the hard way. You need to be brave enough to hold the line and fight for your business every time you order supplies, release a new product, add a new employee, or make payroll. It takes guts to stand your ground and defend your dream, not as a daydream but as the incarnation of your life's assets and opportunities.

When the Spartan hoplites left for war, the women and old folks back home sent them off with this admonishment: "Spartan! Come back with your shield or on it!" If they came back with it, they had held the line in battle, not tossing aside their armor and weapons as they ran away. If they came back on it, they were being returned with honor, having fought well and died. It was that courage, that commitment to never surrender, which is remembered in two famous lines from the Battle of Thermopylae. Three hundred Spartans held a narrow pass, blocking an army of hundreds of thousands of Persians. When asked to lay down their weapons, they replied, "Come and get them." When told that the Persians would fire so many arrows it would block out the sun, the Spartans answered, "Good, then we shall fight in the shade."

Entrepreneurs need to be that kind of brave, to have temerity. They know that if they won't stand and fight for their business, no one else will. The faint of heart need not apply.

C IS FOR CLEVER

When I started making this alphabetical list, my first draft had "C is for Creative."

But the more I thought about it? No. Creativity is overrated—and I say that as someone who has made his living as a creative. But it's true. And, while I'm at it, vision is overrated, too. Being creative, visionary, and imaginative is obviously *important* for an entrepreneur, but not as important as everyone seems to think.

Given a choice, I think entrepreneurs are better off being clever and shrewd than creative or visionary. If I were betting on startups, I'd certainly bet on the clever, shrewd businessman over the creative visionary. Of course, the creative might win sometimes, but the odds favor the shrewd entrepreneur. Intelligence, imagination, creativity, vision, education: these are all valuable qualities for anyone starting a business. But being clever is essential, even indispensable. Here are some other indispensable entrepreneurial traits that start with C: *crafty, canny, cunning, calculating.* The entrepreneur ought to be "street smart." A clever business owner can go a lot farther with average creativity and a pedestrian vision than an imaginative genius without any street smarts. Read that last sentence again. Is there any real doubt that it hasn't been proven right millions of times in the harsh conditions of the real world? You can become a millionaire by shrewdly launching a chain of laundromats. Most of my writer, musician, and artist friends can't figure out how to get paid for what they do.

Remember the Trojan War? The Greeks had been camped on the beach in front of the ancient city of Troy for ten years. It was a stalemate, an unbreakable siege. The Trojan walls were too strong and the Greeks had terrible leaders. Agamemnon and Achilles fought over a girl; other leaders were too vain to be effective. Still others were lazy, or too superstitious to take risks. Some were

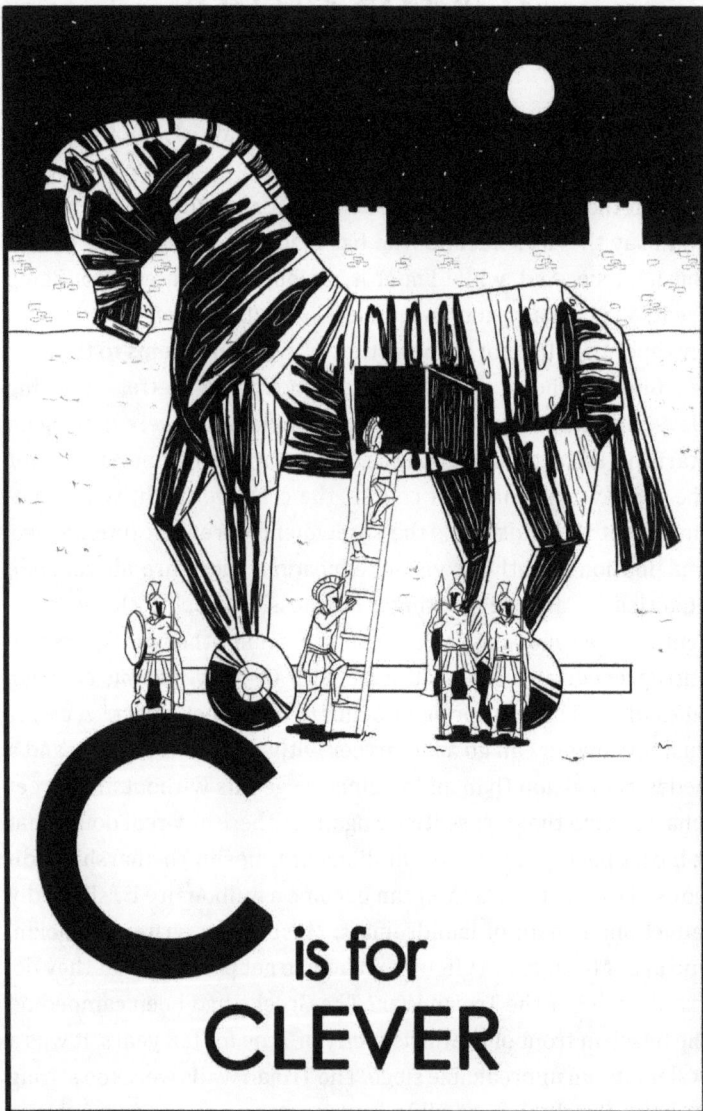

C is for
CLEVER

brilliant fighters or military tacticians, but none of them could figure out how the heck to get past Troy's walls. So for ten years they just sat in their tents by their ships, drinking wine, boasting, listening to minstrels, and making love to their concubines.

But there was one Greek war chief who was different. He wasn't the best fighter, didn't command the biggest regiment, and didn't have the best political connections. But by the gods, Odysseus was a canny, cunning, conniving schemer who became a hero to the Greeks for always thinking his way out of a jam. The Greeks considered Hercules the national hero who most embodied strength, and Theseus the hero who most embodied virtue and intelligence, but it was Odysseus who best embodied cleverness—and the Greeks *loved* cleverness.

Odysseus came up with a trick. Since they couldn't breach the walls by force, perhaps they could sneak in with a street-smart scheme—you might even say a scam. He knew that the Trojans, being from Asia Minor, loved and worshipped horses. So he had the Greeks build a giant wooden horse and leave it on the beach as if it were an offering to the gods. Then they got into their ships and put out to sea. From the tops of their walls, the Trojans saw the Greek war galleys sail over the horizon. They came out and started to party (they'd been cooped up for ten years). They ran down to the beach to check out what was left of the Greek camp. *Whoa! A giant wooden horse! The Greeks must have left it as an offering for the gods—it's an omen! Let's drag it into the city and then the gods will be pleased with us!*

So they dragged the horse into the city square and proceeded to party some more. They got drunk and fell asleep. In the middle of the night, a few Greek soldiers, led by Odysseus, opened a trapdoor in the horse's belly where they'd been hiding and jumped out. They unlocked the gates and the Greek army, which had just sailed a few miles down the coast, came inside and pillaged and burned the city. Problem solved.

I can already hear you saying, "But Odysseus *was* creative: the horse trick was genius! He had vision." Sure, I'm not saying that creativity doesn't help. But Odysseus wasn't trying to be creative;

he was trying to *solve the problem*. Cleverness was the driver, creativity just the means.

I meet a lot of would-be entrepreneurs who aren't clever enough. They might be intensely creative, deeply intelligent, highly educated, and have a great idea for a product. Some have fantastic resumes with accomplishments and experience in some very large companies. What they lack is a sort of street-level cunning about how to sell things to make a profit.

That's why I think that entrepreneurs who start running small businesses at the street level have an advantage. People who go straight from college into an MBA program and then to work for a very large corporation and climb to upper-middle management have missed some important lessons in entrepreneurship, no matter how educated or creative they might be. They never earned the shrewdness that comes by starting at the bottom—running a taco shop, learning how to hustle, how to play the angles, and how to keep cash flowing and products being delivered. The marketplace is a Darwinian jungle, red in tooth and claw. The clever figure it out: how to make a buck or two in it, how to survive, how to come out on top. Those who don't? Well, they don't.

Being clever means being resourceful. I love this quote by Robert Heinlein. It's like an entrepreneur's job description:

> *"A human being should be able to change a diaper, plan an invasion, butcher a hog, conn a ship, design a building, write a sonnet, balance accounts, build a wall, set a bone, comfort the dying, take orders, give orders, cooperate, act alone, solve equations, analyze a new problem, pitch manure, program a computer, cook a tasty meal, fight efficiently, die gallantly. Specialization is for insects."*

The entrepreneur needs to be clever and competent, a human Swiss Army knife that solves problems and gets stuff done. In starting a business, I think that trumps creativity or intelligence or imagination. Show me a highly creative, highly intelligent, highly educated individual, and I'll meet him or her for a lively conversation at the pub. But if someone has *only* those qualities and starts a business competing against someone who's clever and came up from the streets? I'll still meet the creative person, but I'm guessing I'll have to buy the round.

D
is for
DECISIVE

D IS FOR DECISIVE

January 15, 2009, was an ordinary Thursday in New York City. At LaGuardia Airport, the usual mix of mid-week travelers boarded US Airways Flight 1549. It was a typical business run scheduled to stop in Charlotte and continue on to Seattle.

The sky was clear as US1549 taxied to the end of Runway 4. At 3:25 p.m. it accelerated toward the northeast. As the Airbus A320 cleared the tarmac and began its climb, passengers with window seats on the left could see the skyline of Manhattan, just three or four miles away across the East River.

Two minutes later, as the plane was passing through an altitude of 2,700 feet on its initial climb to 15,000 feet, the first officer noticed a flock of Canada geese flying toward the aircraft. Eleven seconds after that, when the plane was at an altitude of 2,818 feet, the flock collided with the Airbus. The cockpit windshield turned dark and several loud thuds could be heard against the fuselage. More ominously, there were several loud bangs inside the engines as large birds were sucked into the intakes. Both engines flamed out almost immediately.

At once, 1549 began losing power. It continued to climb briefly, but the airspeed began dropping rapidly. Unless corrective action was taken, the aircraft would go into a stall. It was four-and-a-half miles north of LaGuardia, and had reached 3,060 feet over the ground at 185 knots per hour. That was as high and fast as 1549 would go that day.

The pilot in command was Captain Chesley B. "Sully" Sullenberger. Fifty-seven years old, Sullenberger was a United States Air Force Academy graduate who had flown fighter planes before leaving active duty in 1980. As of January 15, 2009, he had logged 19,663 flight hours in his career. To put that into context, that's 820 twenty-four hour days—the equivalent of being at the controls for two full years, 24/7, 365. He had 4,765 hours in just the Airbus A320 aircraft. He was also a safety expert and glider pilot. In other words, the best possible man for the job was in charge that day.

When one listens to the audio communications between the cockpit and LaGuardia air traffic control (which is easily found on the web), three things stand out. First, it all happened very, very, quickly. The flight was over just a few minutes after the bird strike, and Sullenberger had only seconds to make his decisions. Second, his voice was calm and dispassionate. It was the voice of a confident uberprofessional. Third, Sullenberger was decisive. He made rapid decisions in real time based on the best information available to him. He didn't equivocate, second-guess himself, agonize, or change his mind. He processed the data in front of him, decided, and acted without doubt or hesitation.

He quickly realized that he didn't have the speed or altitude to pull a U-turn and make it back to any of the LaGuardia runways. He asked if Teterboro Airport, across the river in New Jersey, might have a clear runway. The air traffic controller told him that they would clear a runway at Teterboro for him, but within seconds Sullenberger realized that at his rate of descent, with less than 3,000 feet underneath him, he'd never make it that far. There are perhaps two or three seconds in which you can almost hear Sullenberger mentally checking off his options. He then *told* (he didn't ask) air traffic control that he would be ditching the plane into the Hudson River, right next to the towers of midtown Manhattan. The air traffic controller asked for clarification, as if he couldn't believe what he was hearing, and then acknowledged Sullenberger's decision.

After that, there wasn't much communication. The flight crew was working to bring the aircraft down to land on its belly on top of the water, which at that speed would be as hard as concrete but far more turbulent and with much more drag. Even the smallest misalignment would cause the airframe to tumble across the waves.

But that isn't what happened. Sullenberger landed the A320

right onto the Hudson River. There was no tumble, no crash, no sinking, and not a single death or serious injury. One hundred fifty-five souls were picked up by rescue boats and walked off the docks to safety.

It's often said that starting a company is like building an airplane while flying it. That's an excellent analogy. The entrepreneur rarely has the luxury of figuring it all out and getting it all right before launch. And every new business has all sorts of crises like the bird strike that almost killed the 155 passengers and crew on 1549. It's not *if* a new company will face emergencies, but when.

And when it does happen, the entrepreneur must be decisive. There is no time to freak out, hesitate, second guess, or reverse course. The successful entrepreneur takes in the data, processes it, and acts—like Captain Sullenberger.

Sometimes, like Sullenberger, entrepreneurs make the right decisions, pull off a miracle, and save their company and employees. Sometimes they don't. But that's the difference between success and and failure, isn't it? It's not always fair, but there are no mulligans or do-overs or retests. When something breaks, a key employee quits or goes to work for a competitor, your product starts blowing up, the cash runs out, etc., you have to make decisions decisively and act on them definitively. What you decide and how you act on it will probably determine if you will be an entrepreneur who successfully started a company or just someone who tried, but crashed and burned before you got too far from the airport. That's harsh, but real.

The hardest decisions most entrepreneurs will have to make concern money and people. Hiring, firing, buying, paying, selling, asking, borrowing, partnering—for the entrepreneur, all of these happen to and through and by people. Getting money, spending money, saving money, budgeting money—all of these issues have faces and relationships attached to them. You say *yes* or *no* to people. You hire someone new and show someone close to you the door. These would be hard enough decisions if they were just case-study examples in a business school classroom. But for the entrepreneur, in the life of the startup, these are emotional decisions that give you little time to ponder or panic. Like Captain Sullenberger, your startup company doesn't have a lot of altitude or airspeed. If you want to own the money and the glory of success, you have to own the hard and fast choices it will take to survive, much less thrive.

I like what Robert Heinlein said: "When the need arises—and it does—you must be able to shoot your own dog. Don't farm it out—that doesn't make it nicer, it makes it worse." I've had to fire someone who really needed the job, knowing that they were going to go home to a life and family thrown into chaos, and that it would create havoc in our workplace and in my world. Every entrepreneur has. Like Sullenberger evaluating whether he could make a U-turn back to LaGuardia, make it across the river to Teterboro, or ditch in the Hudson, we have to ask ourselves how much altitude and airspeed our companies have and what has to be done to keep them from crashing. And then we have to act decisively.

This is less a management technique than a personality or character trait. You are either a decisive individual or you aren't. If you aren't, you need to figure out if you can become one. That might mean significant character development and training. If you have to, then you'd better get started now or get out of the startup business. You never know when the next bird might strike.

E IS FOR ENERGETIC

It's just the weirdest thing: I seem to run into a lot of wannabe entrepreneurs with the bizarre notion that if they start a business they'll be able to work *less* than they do now. They daydream about starting a company as a path toward an easy-going, latte-at-the-coffee-house-in-the-morning, craft-beer-in-the-afternoon, creatively-chilling-while-talking-about-innovations-over-tapas lifestyle. The small-business startup community is full of people who *hate* working for someone else—who even hate the *idea* of working for someone else—and have bought the be-the-boss daydream hook, line, and sinker.

This is as clearly as I can say it: being your own boss gives you the freedom to manage your own time, but is so demanding that unless you choose to actually work more and harder than you did in a traditional job, you're going to fail. Anyone who tells you that you're going to succeed more by working less either 1) doesn't know what he or she is talking about, or 2) is lying to sell you something (multilevel marketing, materials on how to get rich without working, etc.).

Being an entrepreneur requires an awful lot of energy. You have to get up early, work long days, not slouch, not slack. If you don't pay attention to what's going on, even for a day or two, things will begin to fall apart.

And that brings up another E-word: *entropy*. It's the tendency in the physical world for things to fall apart on their own. Actually, it's the Second Law of Thermodynamics. It teaches us that the universe tends to become disordered over time. Energy runs down and organization decays. You can tidy up your room, but it will fall apart. You can put money in your bank account, but it will dribble out. You can organize your employees, but they will gradually fall into chaos. Entropy is constantly clawing at the uni-

E is for
ENERGETIC

verse, and it is constantly clawing at your business. Entropy can only be countered with more energy. Entrepreneurs always need to be putting more energy back into their business than entropy is draining out of it. That's an ongoing battle, like water draining out of a leaky tub that can't be patched—only steadily adding more water keeps you ahead of the loss. Or it's like bailing out a leaking boat: you have to stay ahead of it by bailing it out faster than it's coming in. Businesses are like that: they're constantly falling apart. Employees are always becoming disorganized, disheartened, discouraged, or distracted; customers are falling away to competitors; money is flowing out unless you keep making more. The entrepreneur has to be energetic enough to overcome the entropy eating away at the company.

So, what does it look like for entrepreneurs to be energetic? They have to wake up every day and have three kinds of energy:

1. **Physical Energy.** This is just too hard of a job if you are a low-energy individual. If you sleep late, want a nap in the afternoon and to wind down early, then being an entrepreneur might not be for you. You've got to have a lot of physical energy to get up early, keep moving, and stay up late when necessary.

2. **Intellectual Energy.** You need to be curious, think fast, process data, and keep track of a lot of information. Operations, production, human resources, accounting, marketing, sales, and government compliance are just some of the thousand things you have to keep up with. If you don't have a lot of intellectual or mental energy, you won't be able to stay ahead of the entropy.

3. **Emotional Energy.** Your emotions are also subject to entropy. There are days when you will come in and it will seem like you're losing more than you're winning, like you're taking one step forward but sliding back two or three. Deals fall apart, employees quit, unexpected expenses come up. *Sigh. Depression. Anxiety. Fear.* How will you counter that?

I have a friend who owns a successful restaurant. I love to hear him talk about his work because I find the restaurant business endlessly fascinating. It's a microcosm of every business challenge. A restaurateur has to do everything: production, purchasing: hiring/firing, HR, marketing, sales, bookkeeping. It demands mastering all sorts of business skills. There's a relentless pace, from prep to waves of customers. After the evening service, you close and do your counts, clean up, turn off the lights, and the next day you get up to face a whole new set of customers. It gives you the opportunity to reinvent it every day.

I like to play golf with this guy and pick his brain about business. He gets home at two o'clock in the morning and lays awake making his lists for tomorrow. Entropy is constantly clawing at the restaurant. Equipment, like the big commercial refrigerators, could break down and thousands of dollars of food could go bad overnight. Busboys drop plates and glasses. Product is always getting less fresh: the fish entrees have to sell because you can't store them overnight. Entropy pulls at the employees. Line cooks and waitresses come and go, with all sorts of personal problems that keep them from showing up on time. Others call in sick on busy evenings or quit at the worst moments. My friend's restaurant probably has fifty or sixty employees, and to keep them all organized and working together takes constant energy on his part. Entropy also affects the customers: there's always a new restaurant opening in town, so he has to keep marketing and providing exceptional service, even to his regulars. His restaurant is constantly on the edge of breaking down if he doesn't attend to it every single day. It can never be on autopilot: if he takes his eye off the ball for a week it would start to disintegrate.

Starting a business is not a better job, it's a different kind of life. It has the potential for enormous rewards, but it comes with great costs. Choose carefully, because once you jump into this pool, it's very difficult to climb back out.

F IS FOR FRUGAL

Worthwhile pilots and sea captains know their vessels intimately. They know every weld, every system, every rattle and hum coming from the engines. They know every instrument and what those instruments are telling them. They can feel the vital essences—fuel, oil, hydraulic fluid, electricity—flowing through the veins of their aircrafts or ships. When something is amiss, they react decisively because they can see in their mind what the problem is and what their options are.

Any business owner worth his or her salt knows where every penny in the business is, every day, and how it got there. Money is the blood of a business, its life force, and the purpose of its existence. A business owner who doesn't pay attention to the money, who can't read the balance sheet or the cash flow report, cannot truly lead the organization or react to problems when they arise. Owners who can't follow the money become ex-owners.

I could have called this chapter "Fiscally Responsible." That might even more accurately describe what I'm getting at, but it too easily lends itself to confusion and self-deception. Responsibility is a slippery concept—responsible to what or whom? Irresponsible entrepreneurs never think of themselves as irresponsible; they consider themselves visionary or risk-taking or clever, playing a game that makes sense to them even if it doesn't to anyone else. Frugality gets a bad rap, but it doesn't have to mean cheap or risk-averse—some of history's most successful investors were frugal. So, I'm going with frugal because it implies that the owner knows the value of every dollar and doesn't part with it without really understanding the potential return. Frugal entrepreneurs have their eyes wide open. They remember Benjamin Franklin's advice: "Beware of little expenses; a small leak will sink a great ship." They know you can't leak money, or lose a little bit on every

F
is for
FRUGAL

sale, and make it up in volume. They are awake and aware.

Because money is the blood in the veins of a business, if you really want to understand a business, follow its money. Every company has a thousand critics who think they know how it works, or how it should work. It's easy to stand outside on the sidewalk and opine about why a company does what it does or what it ought to do. But unless you're inside, seeing and really grasping the money part—how it's made and where it goes—you will never understand that business or be able to offer an intelligent critique of it. Everything revolves around revenue and returns. A business's best and worst qualities can usually be explained and predicted by the flow of its cash.

I've heard employees pound their chests and say that the owner they work for doesn't really understand the company because he or she doesn't know what it's like to perform some function on the shop floor. But employees and the jobs they do are like organs in the body. The money that flows to and from each body part explains why and how and how long that organ will function within the system. The CEO may not know how to do your job, but if you don't see how the money flows, you will never understand his. To be blunt, owners who don't grasp the money part of their business won't be owners for long. An entrepreneur must always know where the cash is going to come from, how much of it there is, and where it's going.

On the other hand, worry about money pierces the heart, corrodes the mind, and makes life taste sour. It leads to all sorts of grief and evil. There's a common misunderstanding that the Bible says that money is the root of all evil. The actual quote is much more accurate and chilling. It's in 1 Timothy 6, verses 9-10:

"Those who want to get rich fall into temptation and a trap and into many foolish and harmful desires that plunge people into ruin and destruction. For the love of money is a root of all kinds of evil. Some people, eager for money, have wandered from the faith and pierced themselves with many griefs."

How do you meet the financial demands of entrepreneurship without allowing it to pierce you with many griefs? Some people are able to balance frugality, business acumen, and ambition with generosity, temperance, and humility. It's how they are wired; probably a product of both nature and nurture, and a lot of cultivated skills. From what I've seen, some people figure it out: they run growing businesses but find ways to lower their overhead to reduce stress and give themselves some room to maneuver. They earn and save more, want and spend less. They give more. They master the money part so it doesn't master them.

Just another quick point that may or may not apply to you, but I see enough of it it's worth mentioning. I spend a lot of time working around people who want to launch businesses as platforms for nonprofit work. I think that's wonderful, admirable, and responsible. I hope that so many people buy this book that I will have extra resources to contribute to causes that I believe in.

But beside that, I'm deeply concerned for a lot of these people because I fear they are setting their business up for failure. Your business model cannot be just a means to an end, or it will never work. No, the goal in life is not to get as rich as we can. But a business that sees its core activity as just overhead to its supposedly "real" purpose is working against itself.

Whether you build cars, design flower gardens, or sell lemonade from a stand in front of your parent's house, ninety-nine per cent of owning a business is selling something for more money than it costs to make it. It really is that simple. If that's not for you, don't start a business.

You might want to be socially responsible and change the world. So do I. But you also have to be honest with yourself and others: if you don't really want to run a business, then don't. But don't waste yours and other peoples' time, money, and opportunities on something that your heart isn't really in. You won't be doing yourself, your employees, or your customers any good by only pretending to care about what you're doing. If you really want to work for a nonprofit, then go do that.

If you're going to be an entrepreneur, you need to tell yourself the truth about yourself. The reality is that some people can handle the money part without it eating them up and destroying them, and some can't. Some people like to deal with money and are good at it, and some don't and aren't. Some people get very emotional about money, and some don't. Some people are energized by solving financial problems, and some are drained and depressed. Whichever kind of person you are by default, however you were born or wired from the womb, hear and know this: an entrepreneur has to mess with money and figure out finances every day. Every. Single. Day.

Because cash flow is the lifeblood of a business, it's your blood if you own it. You live or die by it whether it keeps flowing. If you aren't a money person, then you'd better become one fast—real fast. As in, *the-first-day-you-decide-that-you're-an-entrepreneur* fast. From that day on, the beating heart of that business and the cash that flows through its veins are, or should be, on your mind every day. If you don't like thinking about and dealing with money, turn around now. Every day you will have to figure out how to make more of it than you spend. If that's not who you are, or you can't grow into that, you might not be cut out to be an entrepreneur.

G is for
GRACEFUL

G IS FOR GRACEFUL

Fred Astaire and Ginger Rogers had one of the most famous onscreen partnerships of the 1930s and 40s. It was the great age of the musical, and many movies were vast, panoramic extravaganzas. Characters would break out singing and dancing in elaborate set pieces. During the Great Depression and World War II, it was probably refreshing to go to the movies and see beautiful people moving elegantly in gorgeous costumes on lavish sets. Fred and Ginger were the king and queen of the musicals because they were world-class dancers. Fred Astaire was amazing, with iconic performances like his signature number in *Singing in the Rain.* He was accomplished in jazz, tap, swing, ballroom—he could do it all. In fact, Fred Astaire was such a dance icon that after the war years he lent his name to a national chain of dance schools. Everyone wanted to learn to dance like Fred.

Ginger Rogers was certainly a star, but Fred always got the top billing. That was too bad, because it obscured an important truth about Ginger. I don't know who, but someone once said that, "Ginger Rogers did everything Fred Astaire did, but backwards and in heels." Through all those elaborate routines, dancing cheek-to-cheek, up and down stairs, around big props, Ginger matched Fred step-for-step but with a higher difficulty rating. Ginger made it look easy. She glided, elegance in motion. She was graceful.

The dictionary defines graceful as "elegance or beauty of form, manner, movement, or speech." A few people make very difficult things look easy. Great athletes dunk a basketball, ski a slalom course, hit a pitch, catch a pass, or swing a golf club in a way that doesn't look awkward, forced, or even difficult. They make us think that we might be able to do it ourselves, and so we go out to the hoop in our driveway or the local ski hill and imagine that we look just as effortless. But this sets us up for disappointment.

The graceful professional performance has convinced us that it's supposed to be *easy* to effortlessly swing a sand wedge, pitch the ball fifty yards, and stick it next to the pin. We see ourselves doing it like the pros on TV as we stand there in the sand trap on Saturday afternoon at our local course. Then we take a hacking swing and watch the ball go six yards from the trap into the weeds. Then we hack again and it goes into the pond. We get angry because we have grand visions of graceful performers who execute perfect shots while looking like they're not even trying very hard.

Really gifted entrepreneurs sometimes make their businesses look effortless. Ordinary people like you or I watch videos of them at some conference and get inspired. Then we start companies, assuming that we'll gracefully innovate, launch incredible products at a great profit, take off like a rocket, get written up in magazines, and tell our amazing stories at conferences. A few entrepreneurs are exquisitely good at that special thing that they do. They've cultivated their God-given abilities with acquired skills, pulling it all together with hard work and perfect timing. But what we see from a distance might not really be very easy at all. These folks just make it *look* easy because they have grace.

There are a couple of lessons we need to learn:

1. **Gracefulness is closely associated with success.** Unremarkable performers will rarely be described as "graceful." We need to be honest with ourselves and admit that if our work or performance isn't graceful, we might need more practice. The "Ten Thousand Hour Rule" reminds us that it takes approximately ten thousand hours of repetitive experience to really perfect a skill. When we watch great entrepreneurs at the top of their game launch products or businesses like Ginger Rogers dancing backwards, we need to remember that we never saw all their years of practice or the failures along the way. If we're still clunky and awkward in our entrepreneurial efforts, we might need to log more time (maybe a lot more) and be willing to fail (maybe more than a few times).

2. **Gracefulness doesn't just impress, it can inspire.** If we can get good enough to make it look easy, others will feel an instinctive attraction and an inclination to follow us. It's only natural to want to be on a team supporting a graceful performer. Grace lets us inspire our followers and makes everyone around us look a little better. And that inspiration translates to investment, making it easier to sell our business plan or products to fans, customers, and venture capitalists. The graceful entrepreneur makes it look easy to recruit great employees, so the more fluid you can be, the better team you can build.

But there's another definition of the word grace. It can also mean showing kindness or mercy to someone who doesn't deserve it. In that sense, grace is when someone gets what they need, not what they deserve. Entrepreneurs should consider being graceful in this sense as well, especially as they rise in the business world. If you make too many enemies on your way up, you won't have enough friends when you really need them. To be honest, many of the most successful entrepreneurs notoriously never cut anyone an inch of slack. Some of our greatest business heroes (Steve Jobs, for example) were famous for being hard on everyone they worked with and considered this the secret to their success.

Much of the time you do have to be pretty hard-nosed and thick-skinned. You have to be willing to fire people, drive a tough bargain, and uphold high standards. But on the other hand, if you go through your business career routinely alienating and damaging the people around you, burning bridges and leaving bodies in your wake, you may go far but eventually face a certain karmic justice. Every action has an equal and opposite reaction, and consequences catch up with you. The truth floats. If you are an ungraceful person, you may find yourself getting no grace when it's your turn to need some. To reach your goals you might need to give some ground, enlist some allies, or even make some friends along the way. Some of our entrepreneurial "heroes" left behind great products, world-changing companies, and a lot of hurting people. People remember them as great businessmen but lousy human beings. As you plan your entrepreneurial career, you need to think long and hard about who you want to be and what you want to leave behind. Those are among the most important questions any of us will ever wrestle with. As you do, especially in our win-at-all-costs business culture, you might consider Jesus' question: "What does it profit a man to gain the whole world and lose his own soul?"

H IS FOR HEALTHY

Business is battle.

That cliché turns off half the people who hear it. They believe it frames entrepreneurship as a combative, zero-sum game. In their minds, building a business means collaboration, diplomacy, and the ability to discover ways for everyone to win.

But I'm going to stand by my battle analogy. Business is a life-or-death competition, if not for the owner, at least for the business itself. If it doesn't win, it can die. It has competitors and antagonists that can certainly seem like (or actually become) enemies. The life of a business is full of unexpected crises and outright attacks. Like a war, starting a business will drain a treasury, cause untold stress, require rapid reaction, push leaders to the limits of their endurance, and has to be understood on both the strategic and tactical levels. And while great commanders do collaborate and build teams, they do so as a means to winning.

It would be easy to say entrepreneurship is a marathon, but it's much harder than that. A marathon is hard (I ran one once, and I remember), but it's a struggle with limited dimensions: you move in a more or less straight line, mile-markers measure your progress to a defined finish line, competitors don't attack you, and it's reasonably achievable if you prepare properly and stay within your limits for a few hours. But starting a business has none of those advantages. The route isn't marked. You don't know where the finish line is (or even if there is one) or how far along you are toward it. You're subject to unpredictable challenges, attacks, and betrayals. There are no proven training plans. You're constantly having to sprint or slow down, moving outside your comfort zone just in order to survive. Entrepreneurs get beaten, bruised, betrayed, and busted up all along the way. Starting a company will test you mentally, emotionally, and physically. You'll have to solve

H is for HEALTHY

problems, deal with disappointment, and work long hours while eating poorly. Entrepreneurs face late nights and early mornings, physical labor, disturbed sleep, inconsistent diets, and anxious days waiting for responses to proposals or for cash flow to come through.

In this battle, entrepreneurs need good health to survive, much less thrive. I haven't heard too much conversation about this in the startup community because it's socially impolite, but it lies just below the surface in many of our judgments about entrepreneurs: we feel more confident when they appear physically fit, mentally sharp, and emotionally composed. We're certainly more likely to invest in or accept a pitch from someone who projects healthy confidence than one who seems fragile in body, mind, or spirit.

Medical science is developing a better grasp of the mind-body connection. It turns out that a lot of the behaviors we associate with startups—disturbed sleep patterns, high stress, inconsistent diet and exercise, travel, emotional pressure, etc.—have a severe impact on our bodies. The inverse is true as well. It turns out that generations of drill sergeants and gym teachers were right: weak bodies really do lead to weaker minds and less emotional resilience. And as much as technology aids productivity, it makes our bodies sicker, our minds weaker, and our emotions more fragile.

Bottom line: starting a business is a battle that will take a real toll on your body, mind, and heart. There's not much you can do to prevent that, so you'd best prepare for it by being as healthy as you can.

Let me get personal. As a creative, I learned to cram in college. I discovered a formula for success: near-toxic levels of stress, adrenaline, caffeine, intuition, and inspiration produced a creative high that was like another gear as I wrote the paper or edited the film (I studied photojournalism and film). My brain and body got into the "Zone," a sort of frenetic alternative state, and the words and images just flowed. I had insights and ideas in the wee hours before a morning deadline that never came during normal work in the weeks before. It did the trick: professors gave me As and said my work was brilliant. Like some perverse behavioral science experiment, I got rewarded for unhealthy behavior, which only reinforced it. I came to depend on it as a method. And I know I'm not the first or last to stumble on this secret. Today, even the best and brightest college students are popping Adderall or other dangerous stimulants to gain an edge.

After college, I made a career out of this trick. And like a performing dolphin in a show at SeaWorld, I kept getting a fish when I did it. I thought I did my best work through these unhealthy, maybe even unholy, practices. And so I gravitated toward work that allowed me to do my thing. I hated the thought of plodding through a project in an office. People close to me would accuse me of procrastinating, of writing the speech on the plane to the conference or the report in the hotel bar the night before the presentation because I knew I could get away with it. But that wasn't quite right: I did it that way because the adrenaline rush honestly produced my best work. I didn't know how to do it any other way. If I burned the candle at both ends, it was a home run. The audience, readers, or clients would give me raving reviews. If I chipped away at it for a month, the product was dull and plodding.

But there are no free lunches. Burning myself out came at a real cost. My body broke down in various ways. My brain performed faster and better than most of my competitors—that's why I won—but while I hyper-focused on the project, everything else became sloppy. I couldn't remember the details of ordinary life: bills to pay, phone numbers, appointments, birthdays. After the project was over, the speech delivered, the manuscript published, I crashed hard by watching stupid TV or playing video games for hours and days. I was a one-trick pony: I could perform my act at a very high level, but not much else. My health, my relationships, and my emotional state all suffered.

Why am I sharing this? Because I think a lot of entrepreneurs are like me. We run on adrenaline. Stress and pressure raise our game and produce our best work. We love competition and risk and the challenge of proving in the arena of our business that we're smart, innovative, unpredictable winners. We start businesses because we *need* this. We can't plod along in our career, working for someone else. The risk/reward equation doesn't frighten us. God help us, it turns us on.

But it isn't free: our bodies, brains, and souls pay a price. Those who love and endure us pay a price. Our accounts are finite, our bodies have limits. Our brains lose their resilience over time. Our emotions can stretch only so far before they don't snap back into shape after the deadline.

If only this *was* a marathon: run for a few hours and get a commemorative t-shirt and beer. That's recreation. But this is a battle, and if you're on an unsustainable path you won't survive. What can't go on, won't. There are so many examples of entrepreneurs building billion-dollar businesses and wrecking themselves in the process that it's become a cliché.

We need your entrepreneurship. We need you to invent and innovate and invest the stuff of your life into brilliant products and great companies. To be brutally honest, that's going to stress every aspect of your being. That's just the way it is. People who want safety and ease without risk, stress, and a crushing workload shouldn't bother being entrepreneurs. But knowing that this is what you signed up for, please do everything you can to stay healthy while you do it. Take care of your body, including your brain. And guard your heart, learning the wisdom of managing your emotions and cultivating your soul. Maybe there is a finish line ahead for your startup—who knows? But until then you're in for a long, tough haul. Do everything you can to be healthy long enough to stay in the game and make your life worth living along the way.

is for
IMPRESSIVE

I IS FOR IMPRESSIVE

My first thought was to call this chapter "I is for Inspiration-al." The business literature and startup conferences go on and on about how entrepreneurs are supposed to be inspirational lead-ers. It's part of the whole "cult of the entrepreneur" that rose out of the Silicon Valley tech revolution and increasing disenchant-ment with traditional business models. Entrepreneurs are now expected to appear on stages wearing wireless headset mics and roaming around in front of giant screens, "inspiring" investors, followers, and wannabes.

In reality, some entrepreneurs do inspire innovation and vi-sion—but others just inspire fear or antipathy, depending on their politics, cultural tribe, leadership style, etc. Some very successful entrepreneurs are just hardworking nerds or brilliant blue-collar types with great ideas and an instinctive drive to build business-es. They aren't all inspiring in the way that word is usually used. But they all need to be impressive.

Why? Because entrepreneurs have to recruit employees, in-vestors, and customers to take risks with them. Some can do that by casting an inspirational vision, but not all. If you can inspire, great. But the minimum requirement for persuading others to follow you is to impress them with your intelligence, ability, ac-complishments, competence, planning, etc. You'll never get people to buy into your startup if you appear mediocre, or even just av-erage. You have an idea for a new type of grocery store, trucking service, or medical device and you need investors, followers, or early adopters? Well, an inspiring vision is all well and good, but first you need to impress others with your ability to get it done.

How do you create that impression? The best predictor of fu-ture performance is past performance. Before you talk too much about your big idea, show what you've already done. You may be intelligent and gifted in many ways, but what's really impressive is applying those gifts to create a business plan that withstands tough scrutiny. Your demeanor might or might not ooze vision, but it had better convey extreme competence, confidence, and credibility. And make sure that demeanor isn't just a facade.

I remember meeting a guy I'll call Ben. He was six-foot-three and looked like a model. He dressed like a winner. He knew all the latest business startup jargon—he was always dropping words like "velocity" and "flow" into an endless patter about his big ideas. He flew to conferences, name-dropped speakers, and checked all the right apps on his phone. He was "capitalizing" six companies, achieving "strategic alignment" with the right "stakeholders," and was trying to enlist employees to work for stock options instead of salary so he could achieve "speed to market" within his "space."

It was as if Ben had read books and gone to workshops designed to teach someone how to look and sound like an entrepreneur and "cast vision." Which is, coincidentally, exactly what Ben had done. Ben was (in a metaphor for which I will be eternally grateful to Texas), "all hat and no cattle." After you scratched the surface, you discovered that Ben's six companies were all half-baked ideas for which he had done little more than register an LLC and a domain name. Some of them had a product concept or prototype, but none of them were anywhere close to commercial release. The business models were more like schemes that depended on a steady stream of OPM (Other People's Money). Ben was good at pitching banks and investors during the days when they were giving money away with too little oversight. He was also a champ at recruiting idealistic young people desperate to be "inspired" by a "vision" to work for little or no money. But after ten years of running around the startup community creating "buzz," he had not actually created much of anything.

Do you know what genuinely impresses people in an entrepreneur? Not vision, or good looks, or sharp slacks from Banana Republic. It's winning. Winning takes care of everything. Have a string of successes in focused and applicable projects. Don't perpetuate the mistaken notion that success in one field translates to success in another. There are plenty of ex-pro athletes or brilliant academics who couldn't leverage their reputation into starting a successful business. Do you have a great idea for a retail product? Impress prospective investors, employees, and customers with your past winning percentage in retail product sales. Have you made things happen? Have you taken on projects and turned them into winners? Have you shown you know how to keep an enterprise afloat while pleasing customers and turning a profit?

If your answer is, "No, not really," then I guess you ought to think about what you're getting yourself into. Before jumping into the deep end of the entrepreneurial pool, maybe you should get your feet wet and ease into the shallow end. Take the number-two job somewhere to learn and earn your bona fides, or start something small and make it bigger. Otherwise, not only might you fail to impress the helpers you need to launch, you might get in over your head and drown. Starting a successful business is harder than it looks.

Of course, nothing happens if you don't try, and to try you have to start. Which is why I would throw into this mix another I word: *initiative*. Some people are good at getting up and getting started. By definition, entrepreneurs are these kind of people. They don't just sit back and wait until all the stars align or until they can be assured of success. They make things happen by making incremental progress, taking hills, and crossing to-dos off lists. They have impressive initiative.

That being said, initiative comes in at least two flavors: smart and stupid. For example, there are some people who just flail about, jumping stupidly into a series of failed startups. When I go to entrepreneurship conferences, I meet folks who seem to be desperately searching for a way to start anything, any way they can. They want to be an entrepreneur for a lot of reasons, but especially for the impression it will create. Many do so because they've mistaken cause for effect. Entrepreneurs are not impressive just because they are entrepreneurs, it's the other way around: impressive people often turn their considerable talents toward starting a business. The uniform and medals don't make a Marine impressive; they are evidence of impressive accomplishments.

Do you have a winning record in your professional life that you earned by showing initiative, following through, and accomplishing remarkable things? If so, it's likely that you have not only an impressive record but an impressive demeanor. If you want to start a business, you'll need to make use of that reputation, impressing others enough to follow and support you. If you're not that sort of person, you might want to work on building up a track record that you can use to pitch and persuade the people you'll need to build your business.

J IS FOR JUDGEMENTAL

There's hardly any idea more thoroughly pounded into the heads of our schoolchildren today than that being judgmental is bad. Judgmental people are judged to be bad people (the irony of being scathingly judgmental about people for being judgmental seems to escape the intolerant tolerance crowd). It would just be silly if they weren't neutering one of the most critical skills kids will need to survive the fog of life.

If any of those kids aspire to start a business, they'd better learn how to make and stick with accurate judgments, because the career of an entrepreneur is nothing if it's not a series of choices, most made under pressure with inadequate information. Like professional gamblers and the leaders of dangerous expeditions in the Age of Discovery, entrepreneurs live or die by their ability to size up people and products, customers and competitors. They can aspire to make only decisions that are deliberate and data driven—but while they dither, another entrepreneur playing hunches and taking puncher's chances might beat them to the market, or in it.

By definition, start ups are starting—they have no track record, no data from which to project future performance. And, if we were really, truly, brutally honest we'd have to admit that if history allowed business leaders to predict the future—to figure out what products would succeed or flop, what markets would do, what customers really wanted, or how to outmaneuver competitors—then established businesses would almost never stumble or die. But of course they do stumble and die, all the time. Leaders of established businesses seem no better at picking products, predicting markets, or out-thinking their competitors than entrepreneurs with new or newer companies. What the established companies have is more resources, margin, or market share to spend

J
is for
JUDGEMENTAL

or squander covering their mistakes or forcing outcomes.

The history of successful entrepreneurs is famously full of stories of intuitive genius, leaps of logic, lucky guesses, stubborn bets. Some of the greatest shifts in our culture, even our civilization, came through judgmental entrepreneurs. They said *yes* when everyone else said *no,* or *no* when everyone else said *yes*, often without any better reason than gut instinct and a stubborn inability to believe that they could be wrong. According to their biographers, their judgmental natures made them hard to live and work with. They hired and stuck with some people, fired and held irrational grudges against others. Most of them didn't play nice with competitors and they launched products or advertising campaigns because they thought they knew what consumers needed or wanted better than the consumers themselves did. They violated one of the primary values of the tolerance culture: they were sure that they were right and refused to listen to anyone tell them otherwise. And then they backed that judgment up by betting their own futures and fortunes.

We aren't supposed to be judgmental about people. We're supposed to take time, observe, gather information from interaction, work to understand them in context, etc. I'd suggest that's the right way to treat neighbors, friends, and relatives, but entrepreneurs have to start making definitive business judgments about people even prior to launch. From the conception of their start up, the judgmental nature of entrepreneurs is a risk-reward formula, forced upon them by circumstances but hopefully dialed into their DNA as an inherent, useful talent that they have learned to live with and rely upon. For example, many if not most entrepreneurs take on business partners before they make the prototype of their first widget. Most of the time, both partners are young, with no significant resumes or references. Their relationship is a high-stakes gamble. Some of those bets pay billions, and some pay out bankruptcy and bitterness. Sadly, those two outcomes aren't mutually exclusive: too many wildly successful entrepreneurial partnerships end with separations that look more like ugly divorces than the dissolving of business contracts. In the end, the very same judgmental habits of mind that allowed these entrepreneurs to pick partners and form catalytic bonds that built companies can keep them from working through differences later on. Whether it's picking partners, hiring or firing employees, negotiating with clients, forging alliances with other leaders, or taking on investors, entrepreneurs learn to lean on their intuitive (and not entirely rational) judgments. You can tell young entrepreneurs in their twenties to slow down and refrain from making gut-level judgments about people they work with—but good luck getting them to listen. You might as well tell them to slow down and not to be so ambitious or inventive, because intuitive judgment is as much a part of their essential nature as a burning desire to succeed or the ability to come up with new products and services. This is what they do. This is who they are. They are either good at it or they aren't, and their success or failure will largely rest on that distinction.

That's what it comes down to, really. Successful entrepreneurs get used to relying on their intuitive judgments about people because over time they've learned that their instincts are usually right. They learn to listen to their gut. Unsuccessful entrepreneurs also rely on gut instincts about people, but they're wrong often enough to keep them from winning. To put it as simply as possible, some entrepreneurs are good at sizing up people and opportunities, and some aren't—and that's often the margin of victory.

Mistakes can make entrepreneurs doubt their judgment. They start hesitating and equivocating and hedging their bets about people and opportunities. They want more research, more time, less risk. That's perfectly rational, but it's a luxury most entrepreneurs don't have. Start ups move fast. They have to, because markets move fast, driven by fickle consumers and an economy rolling like the deck of a boat. As I said earlier, if more data, time, information, and resources equaled better decision-making about people and products, then big corporations would never make bad hires, fire CEOs, or release products that flop and fizzle. But they do flop and fizzle all the time, while some of the most successful products and partnerships were conceived on a cocktail napkin.

Am I arguing that entrepreneurs should hash out business decisions based on gut instincts on cocktail napkins? No—but they do and they will, more often than they will ever admit. After the fact, to rationalize their decisions to investors, employees, etc., they may tell a story about how much research went into a decision, or they may do research to backstop a judgment they made on gut instinct. They make or break their careers with these leaps of logic. Honesty demands that they (and those around them) be self-aware enough to admit that it's in their nature to bet on their intuition. If a startup were an airplane, there's no computer in the cockpit making decisions based on algorithmic responses to sensor data, but a pilot flying mostly by the seat of his or her pants. For better or worse, you've bought a ticket and boarded this flight. Let's hope he or she has "the Right Stuff" (see the S chapter).

So, what's the take-away here? Should we bless the irrational, intuitive nature of entrepreneurs? It's beyond us to bless or curse it—what difference would that make? It will bless or curse itself by proving right or wrong. But we'd better acknowledge it. Having done so, we should probably factor that into our thinking. If someone has been wrong more often than right about people and situations, should they really be starting a company? Should you invest in or work for someone who's instincts have largely not panned out or outright failed? Is that entrepreneur self-aware enough to own his or her poor judgment, or are they in denial, blaming outcomes on others? Is the entrepreneur with merely average judgment doing anything to improve his or her decision-making skills? Perhaps coaching to learn how to channel their intuition? Learning to listen to advice so they don't hear only their own voice in their head—or gut? Are they learning to delegate some decisions to others with better judgment? Is the entrepreneur healthy enough to rely on their instincts, or are they in a self-deceptive and self-destructive cycle which ought to keep their hand away from the controls?

The entrepreneur never stops making decisions that will affect the business. If you're an entrepreneur, or want to be one, how you react to what you've just read in this chapter is a judgment call that you will have to live with, for better or worse. What are you going to do?

K IS FOR KEEN

In the last chapter, we saw that entrepreneurs are judgmental—meaning they are prone to relying on their intuition, making gut-level, instinctive decisions about people and situations. Some will read that as endorsing ignorant leadership, a license to do dumb things without input. That would be taking the last chapter out of context with the other twenty-five, because each of these qualities forms an integrated personality in the successful entrepreneur. They must also be adaptable, clever, responsible, vigilant, etc.

One of the most important counterweights to the intuitively judgmental nature of entrepreneurs is their keenness. That's not an everyday word for most of us. If we do hear it, it's usually used to mean something like "eager," as in: "I'm *keen* to read Greg Smith's new book." But that's not the primary meaning. The Merriam-Webster Dictionary starts out by defining it as "having or showing an ability to think clearly and to understand what is not obvious or simple about something." Diving a little deeper, the MWD tells us that the word's primary meaning lies in the idea of "sharpness," as in a sharp edge or point. This is usually in the context of saying that someone's mind is sharp ("showing a quick or ardent responsiveness; intellectually alert: having or characteristic of a quick, penetrating mind"). But it's the dictionary's next definition that I want to highlight as it applies to entrepreneurs: "extremely sensitive in perception."

Taking these definitions together, keen has an intimate relationship with the word *observant*. A keen mind is a sharp or penetrating intellect, cutting or seeing through irrelevant distractions and details to recognize the most important information. In fact, keen is often used as an adjective to modify the noun *observer*, as in *a keen observer of human nature; a keen observer of events; a*

K

**is for
KEEN**

keen observer of the market.

Our minds naturally *interpolate* (as opposed to extrapolate): we fill in gaps in our knowledge with supposition. Our brains subconsciously suppose or assume, and sometimes even invent data, in order to make sense out of what we're seeing. Illusionists know how to play on this tendency by misdirecting our attention and fooling our brains into thinking we see something that isn't really there. I had a friend who was professional stage magician. He was bound by the rules of his craft not to reveal secrets, but when we'd watch a famous magician on TV do some baffling illusion, my buddy would smile and subtly direct me to pay attention to something that I missed because the illusionist was misdirecting my attention. Sometimes that was enough to put me on the path to figuring out how the trick worked.

Sherlock Holmes (along with most of the great fictional detectives) was keen: he ignored meaningless or deceptive data to spot clues that others missed. He knew what to look for and what not to look at. Keen minds work that way within their area of expertise.

Attend a cattle auction with an expert rancher and listen to him as he spots which bull to buy—he'll see the qualities you didn't think to look for. Listen to a great football coach evaluate recruits at a tryout or break down plays on video after the game— he'll point out things that you missed because you were looking in the wrong place. Listen to a great entrepreneur talk about product design or consumer preferences—he or she will zero in on tipping-point details in the data that you never would have considered important.

The intuitively judgmental nature of successful entrepreneurs that we talked about in the last chapter is supported by their keenness. They may make a decision on gut instinct, but not in a vacuum. Their gut is telling them things because their eyes have seen clues and their intuition has filtered out the irrelevant facts to focus on what matters most. We all do this to some degree. In a meeting, we're sizing up someone's non-verbal communication—body language, tone of voice, demeanor, what their eyes or hands are doing. We also listen to what they're saying, and sometimes recognize the most interesting phrase or comment buried in a longer dialogue. As the meeting progresses, we're forming judgments about the person and the issue. We have good or bad feelings, or hunches, or little warning lights on the dashboard of our minds. As the meeting draws to a close and we have to decide the question on the table—whether to agree, buy, or hire—we might "go with our gut," but that doesn't mean the decision was completely arbitrary. Below the surface, information was taken in, filtered, processed, and weighed.

The difference between successful and unsuccessful entrepreneurs is often that the good ones are just better at combining keen observation of relevant facts with intuitive judgment. Their hunches are more often right, so their bets pay out more regularly. It might look arbitrary or capricious, but only if we pay attention to judgment and ignore the keen observation that informs it. Entrepreneurs need to have their eyes open, their head on a swivel, and to notice things—often little things others miss or ignore. Human nature is a good example. Entrepreneurs need to be keen observers of people, because people are the key to their success: customers, partners, lenders, employees, competitors. Unless your business is building robots with robots and selling to robots, everything you do has a human element.

This means that most entrepreneurs will face a crisis early in the development of their business because their first partners and hires are often friends, family, or employees that will work for very little. A keen entrepreneur might spot some of their shortcomings and have major misgivings, but still make some bad hires because friends and family are cheap labor. Or they might team up with partners who bring needed cash to the table with strings attached. It's not unusual to hear entrepreneurs later say, "I should have listened to my gut," or, "I knew this was going to be a problem." Hopefully, they grow through the experience. Negative experiences can (but don't always) teach us to be more keenly observant next time, and train us to act on that information by trusting our judgment.

Of course, great entrepreneurs are keenly observant of more

than human nature. Within their area of expertise, they can spot defects in processes or products more quickly than others. They recognize what's really wrong. They see causes, not just symptoms. On the flip side, they can spot the diamond hidden in the coal. Perhaps this is an essential quality buried in a concept, prototype, person, or process that, if developed by stripping away all the irrelevant and unhelpful elements and exposing the core, would turn it into a winner. Successful entrepreneurs make fortunes and change the world with those kinds of keen observations.

Successful entrepreneurs are also keen observers of the environment, and they spot changes in the market more quickly than others. Some sailors can "smell a storm brewing" because of subtle changes in air pressure, shifts in the breeze, or the sea state. Some engineers can tell a machine is going to fail because of subtle changes in the sounds or vibrations it makes, or how much power it's consuming. Great entrepreneurs are keen to what's happening around them. They sense when a market is going to change, when consumers are ready to shift their preferences, when a product is played out and needs to be reinvented, when subtle, seismic shifts in their company's culture indicates that it's time to get ahead of the change that's coming instead of being caught behind it.

There's another K-word that probably fits into this matrix: *kinetic*. Kinetic means energy in motion, and I mention it because keen observation needs to be in fluid motion toward practical action. Professors and pundits might be keen observers of consumers, industries, and markets, but entrepreneurs aren't professors writing books or pundits writing blog posts. The professor or the pundit might have as keen a mind as the successful entrepreneur, but it isn't accompanied by kinetic energy. They see, but don't act. The entrepreneur sees, moves, and gets there first. It reminds me of that famous quote by Wayne Gretzky, perhaps the greatest hockey player of all time. When he retired in 1999 after more than twenty years in the National Hockey Leage, he held or shared sixty-one NHL records, including scoring over one thousand regular season or playoff goals. When asked why he scored so many more goals than anyone else in NHL history, Gretzky said that all the other players saw where the puck was and skated toward it. But he saw where the puck was going to be and got there first. That's the distillation of keen observation, kinetic energy, and intuitive judgment. Successful entrepreneurs master that recipe.

L IS FOR LUCKY

Napoleon Bonaparte shocked Europe like no military leader had since perhaps Julius Caesar. Arising from the blood and ashes of the French Revolution, he made war on the established states of the Continent, destabilizing powers that had held each other in balance for centuries. He won one improbable victory after another by managing to have his forces in the right places at the right times with the right materials to tip battles in his favor. He styled himself an emperor and wielded power in a way that emboldened his troops and unnerved his enemies. If he was in charge, his armies believed they could win and their opponents feared they would lose—the Duke of Wellington, his British nemesis, said that Napoleon's presence on the battlefield was worth 40,000 soldiers.

By all accounts, Napoleon was a remarkable individual, and his unique personality was a key to his success. He wasn't physically imposing (although not as short as legend makes him out to be). But those who met him were struck by his intense and persuasive nature, even with leaders who were strong in their own right.

His critics scoffed at the emperor's accomplishments, writing off his victories as just a string of good luck by lucky generals serving under him. When Napoleon heard that, he responded, "Then give me more lucky generals." Napoleon knew two important truths:

1. Good luck is indispensable to success.
2. You make your own good luck by being prepared to recognize and seize opportunity. As the ancient Roman writer Seneca said, luck is a matter of preparation meeting opportunity.

L is for
LUCKY

Napoleon wanted "lucky" generals working for him because a track record that looked like luck really meant that they had a hard-to-define combination of some of the qualities in this book: successful, decisive, opportunistic, useful, etc. We've been breaking those down to understand them, but when they are working together in a general, or an entrepreneur, they look an awful lot like fortune. Outsiders are tempted to write off winners, whether at war or in the marketplace, as just lucky. The winners themselves know that they won more often than they lost because they increased their probability of victory by preparing to win.

That's exactly what Napoleon did. He had what today we might call an *eidetic* (or photographic) memory—he could almost instantly recall statistics, names, and details about maps, units, supplies, etc. He stayed aware of the latest developments in military technology and had an instinct for how to apply them. He was a gifted manager: organizing finances, logistics, and bureaucracy in complex and interlocking ways to support the war effort. He knew how to issue the right order to the right person at the right time to coordinate efforts, and kept a steady stream of those orders flowing from his office at all hours of the day and night by dictating to multiple secretaries, keeping the puzzle organized in his own mind. He could think ahead, anticipating events and the enemy's moves. He was energetic and healthy, with a powerful work ethic.

In short, Napoleon embodied many, if not most, of the traits in this book. If he had been born at another time and place, he could have been a tremendously successful entrepreneur. But to critics, enemies, and casual observers, he just seemed lucky.

It should be obvious that luck is the apparent aggregate of these qualities: it's been remarked upon many times over the centuries. For example, two of America's founding fathers noted the connection between preparation and luck. Benjamin Franklin said, "Diligence is the mother of good luck," and Thomas Jefferson quipped, "I'm a great believer in luck, and I find the harder I work the more I have of it." Nineteenth-century American poet Ralph Waldo Emerson wrote, "Shallow men believe in luck. Strong men believe in cause and effect."

To sum it up, I'd say that good luck is usually just hard work done in advance, crowned by opportunism and shrewd judgment.

But if consistent "good luck" is an indicator of preparation and judgment, what do we say about the consistently *unlucky* entrepreneur? While everyone has some setbacks that were truly unpredictable, someone who predictably has unpredictable setbacks reminds me of the comic villain Vizzini in the classic movie *The Princess Bride*, who keeps writing off the inevitable failure of every one of his schemes as "Inconceivable!" To which Inigo Montoya epically replies, "You keep using this word, 'inconceivable.' I do not think it means what you think it means." In other words, it was quite conceivable that Vizzini's schemes would fail, but he couldn't or wouldn't anticipate what could go wrong and prepare appropriately.

As an entrepreneur, you need to prepare to be lucky in the same ways Napoleon did.

Prepare by Thinking. Predict the unpredictable, conceive of the inconceivable, and then factor it into your preparations. Do you have the ability to imagine the ways your plans could go wrong and work around them to increase your chances of success? It's a mental skill that grows out of certain habits of mind. A friend of mine who has been a rather successful entrepreneur says that his friends and family are always telling him that he's too skeptical and pessimistic. He responds: "No, I'm just the right amount of skeptical and pessimistic." He seems to see around corners, but of course he doesn't have ESP or clairvoyance. He just imagines the things that could go wrong and fail-safes his plans against those possibilities, at least as much as possible. If you really want to prepare to have good luck, you need to ponder the deep truth of Donald Rumsfeld's (Secretary of Defense under Bush 41 and 43) Three Types of Knowledge until you truly get what they mean, and it changes the way you think and do business. Rumsfeld noted that:

- **There are things we know that we know.** For example, I know that I know what each of my employees makes, and the amount of my average payroll.
- **There are things we know that we don't know.** For example, I know that I don't know who will win the next election and how that might affect my healthcare costs.
- **Then there are the things we don't know that we don't know.** These are always the ones that will bite us in the butt. Every. Single. Time. For example... Well, I can't give you an example, and I can't even think of the questions to ask. But I know there are areas where I'm ignorant of my ignorance, and these are the truly unpredictable variables that might affect my business. All I can do is increase the first two categories of knowledge and try to shrink and contain this one—and to have contingency plans for everything. The American military does this. Every now and then, someone will get a hold of some document from the Pentagon and wave it around on the Internet, claiming that the United States has a secret plan to invade Scotland. Well, of course they do. There are rooms full of people employed to try and minimize this third category (the things we don't know that we don't know) by conceiving of every inconceivable scenario and gaming out contingency plans. I'm sure there are whole file cabinets of plans to be opened in case of the zombie apocalypse, or if Godzilla starts crushing Tokyo (to be fair, those have both been conceived in innumerable films and novels, so we should have them fairly well gamed out). My point is that "lucky" leaders are those who minimized the things they didn't know that they didn't know and were ready when the inconceivable happened.

Prepare by Positioning. My fervent hope is that, in case of the zombie apocalypse or Godzilla rampage, we have troops, tanks, transports, and any manner of other supplies stockpiled and prepositioned to react. That's why there are all of those rooms full of people at the Pentagon writing up plans for how to invade Scotland, just in case we ever have to.

The shrewd entrepreneur has margin built into his time, cash flow, and personnel to react. What if you lose a key employee at a crucial time? What if the cost of a critical supply were to go up in the midst of production? What if a key client went bankrupt in the middle of a deal? What if your partner got hit by a bus, or your computers crashed in the middle of a big project? Predicting the unpredictable is great, but how have you positioned resources to be ready to react?

Prepare by Reacting. We'll talk more about reacting in the N chapter on nimble, but let's just note that when the unpredictable rears its ugly head, you need to react by making adjustments on the fly. That's a lot easier to do if you've thought ahead, built in margins of safety, and stockpiled resources. It's a lot easier to keep calm in a crisis when you're ready, but you still have to react appropriately. That's a developable skill—in fact, emergency workers, pilots, and soldiers rehearse their reactions for just that reason.

Since this appears to have become the Evil Generals Chapter, let me bookend the luck of the bloodthirsty Bonaparte with the shrewd turn of phrase coined by one of the most reprehensible racists in American history. Before he founded the Ku Klux Klan after the Civil War, Nathan Bedford Forrest was a Confederate cavalry officer and a general who won a number of "lucky" engagements. Perhaps the only worthwhile thing history records him saying was his description of how win a battle: "Get there first with the most." In other words, be in the right place (what the U.S. military calls "the decisive point" and an entrepreneur might call the tipping point in the market) at the right time (before your opponent or competitor) with the right resources (overwhelming force or a superior product).

If you can master that, you'll create your own good luck.

M IS FOR MONEYMAKING

There's a whole universe of articles, blog posts, keynote presentations, and college classes waxing lyrical about how the soul of entrepreneurship is innovation, creativity, leadership, teams, social responsibility—yada, yada, yada. Me? I think they're mistaking means for ends.

The classic movie *Patton* (winner of the 1970 Oscar for Best Picture) gave us an unforgettable quote. George C. Scott, playing the blood-and-guts World War II general in an inimitable performance, growls, "Now, I want you to remember that no bastard ever won a war by dying for his country. He won it by making the other poor, dumb bastard die for his country."

In the same spirit, I would say that no entrepreneur ever built a successful business by being innovative, or a great leader, or building super teams, or doing socially responsible work *for its own sake*. He won by innovating, etc. enough to make a profit and take market share from the other poor dumb bastard who didn't.

If that isn't clear enough, let me put it this way: the goal of entrepreneurship is to start a company that makes more money than it spends. All the innovation and leadership stuff is useful to that end, even admirable and heroic—but not the point. If you want to create *for the sake of creating*, take up a hobby. If you want to build teams *for the sake of having great relationships*, start a club. Some things, like contributing to social causes, are *rewards* for starting a profitable business—they're only possible if the business makes more money than it spends long enough to give the owner the luxury of giving some of it away.

In fact, one of the most refreshing things about business is how uncomplicated the object of it is. In a lot of life's endeavors, there's no clear scorecard. How do you know if you're succeeding in something as complex as raising children or running a nonprof-

M is for MONEYMAKING

it ministry? Those are both far more valuable in this life and the next than turning a profit, but not as clearly measurable. My early career was spent in the academic and nonprofit worlds, where collegiality and collaboration were ends. It was all about the process, not the product. It was typical to say something corny like, "The destination doesn't matter, just that we journey together." Suffice it to say that we rarely knew where we were, where we were supposed to be going, how to get there, or if we were making actual progress.

A friend of mine who left full-time ministry had a profound insight after going to work for a manufacturing company. When I was considering reinventing myself and transitioning into the business world, he told me about his epiphany: "Where I work now, the purpose is clear, and so is the scoreboard," he said. "We make car parts and sell them for money. If we sell them for more than it costs to make them, it's good and we get to keep doing it. If it costs more to make them than we can sell them for, it's bad and we don't get to do it for very long. If we lose a little bit on every sale and hope to make it up in volume, we're idiots."

At the end of the day, the entrepreneur goes home with plenty of headaches and heartaches, but he or she also knows the score. Either you're profitable, or on a path to profitability, or you aren't. If you aren't, you're bleeding out—and what can't go on forever won't. Of course, it's obvious that there are seasons in a business when your numbers will be upside-down for a while because you're investing in future growth. There are also seasons when you take an unexpected hit or a calculated risk doesn't pan out. Fair enough. But that doesn't change the object of the game: business is measured by profitability, and the P&L is a scoreboard (if you don't know what a P&L is, you're not ready to start a business). Why else do venture capitalists and bankers all want to see your P&L or tax returns? All the stuff about innovation and leadership is interesting, but only meaningful if it is predictive of putting points on the board.

If all of this sounds unnecessarily harsh and unsophisticated to you, it might be because you aren't a business owner. You might move around the entrepreneurial community, imagining startups, commenting about startups, even starting startups. But if you've been in this game for long, and if you're in it to win it, then you know what I'm saying is true. To be even more blunt, you know I'm right if it's your money on the line. It's all fun and games and innovation and teams while you're gambling with OPM (Other People's Money), as an employee or someone with subsidized funding. When it's yours, it gets really real, really fast.

You may think this mindset is unsophisticated because it's "old school." The new school of startups is, you might think, not tied so tightly to profitability. You might mention some very successful startups that have never turned a profit, like Amazon or Twitter. When I teach on this topic, I always have someone who smirks and tells me my generation doesn't get how business is done today. My response is that the Law of Gravity is a law because it's always true. With enough energy you can get airborne for a while, but you'll never reach escape velocity. What I mean is that any business that doesn't seem to turn a profit is either actually profitable in some way that you don't see, or is creating a debt bubble that will eventually burst.

Besides, it's never wise to base your plans on bizarre exceptions. I had a friend in high school whose parents were both university science professors. This buddy and I got into a bad habit of ditching school to go to the beach during eleventh grade, and the teacher let our parents know that we were in danger of flunking classes. My friend got the parental lecture, and had the poor judgment to argue from an exceptional case: "But Albert Einstein flunked high school math!" To which his mother replied, "Son, I met Dr. Einstein once. And as much as I love you, you are not Dr. Einstein." Lesson: don't excuse your inability to make a profit by referencing some bizarre example from a bubble industry, fueled by billions of dollars of irrational optimism from the investor class—they're pouring money into that company because they expect that, at some point, it's going to put points on the board and win. If that never happens, someone somewhere is going to get fired sooner or later. Don't let it be you.

It's an old cliché to say that you have to spend money to make money, meaning that you might be unprofitable for a season while you invest in growth. But never forget the second half of that sentence: "...to make money." Entrepreneurs take risks. But they never take their eyes off the scoreboard.

N is for NIMBLE

N IS FOR NIMBLE

My dad was an engineer, and when I was a kid he used to tell me that life was like building a bridge. Learn your math, practice your grammar, build your vocabulary. Learn life lessons from sports and part-time jobs. Talk to your school counselor and carefully plan your courses so they align you on a college-prep track. Each career step was like a pier, suspension tower, or girder of a bridge. You look forward and plan, staging the various pieces so the correct one is ready to snap into place at the correct time. Step by well-planned step you span the chasm of chaos that the unprepared and disorganized fall screaming into. I love my father, and I appreciate the wisdom of what he taught me. I confess that I've said similar things to my kids about their education. But the older I get, the less I think that life is a bridge-building exercise. Of all things, I think it's a lot more like a kayak trip.

Imagine that you're kayaking down a deep canyon, with a river zigzagging between steep walls. From your vantage point in the cockpit of your boat, the furthest you can ever see is until the next sharp bend, never more than a quarter mile away. Every time you round a bend, the river presents a new situation for you to react to. It might be full of house-sized boulders, with eddies and back-currents that you need to slalom through. It might be a rushing torrent of whitewater, down a chute or over a series of small waterfalls. Occasionally, it might be a bigger waterfall. Or it might be a smooth stretch of flat water, in which you can set down your paddle and rest while the current carries you along. There might be a beach you can pull aside to camp on, or other kayakers competing with you to thread the obstacles. Obviously, preparation matters: the river will test your skills and equipment. You can't run this river without the right training and tools. But once you've done everything you can to prepare yourself, you have to take the river one bend at a time. You can't plot or rehearse your moves in advance. Every few minutes you get a new set of challenges thrown at you, and you need to react to them in real time. You take the river as it comes.

That's what entrepreneurs have to do. They can and must make business plans. But their plans can only account for what they can see and reasonably anticipate. As we said in the L chapter, they have to try to predict the unpredictable by minimizing the things they know they don't know. After all the contingency planning is done, the margin is built in, and the resources are prepositioned, they will still have to react. They will still have to take the river as it comes, one bend at a time.

Modern entrepreneurs can't just make it up as they go along. They'll never get financed or secure investment if they just wing it all the time. They need plans. But as much as they try to see into the future, they live in the present. Their plans and pitches are written in the future tense ("My company will..."), but they operate in the present tense ("Today we are...").

Entrepreneurs operate in the present tense, but they often make the mistake of spending too much mental and emotional energy on the two things they have the least amount of control over: the past and the future. Obviously, none of us can control, change, or even mildly affect the past. That's why it's called "the past." But behold how we obsess over it! Of course we study past results to better understand current realities and anticipate future outcomes, but we must try to keep our mistakes from becoming albatrosses around our necks (see the R chapter).

Even our control over the future is fairly limited. We can and must plan, prepare, and stack materials for our bridges, but there are so many things that we don't know that we don't know. A tornado can destroy our towers, an economic crisis can steal our funding, an epidemic can strike our workers. A prehistoric monster could rise from the chasm and knock down our bridge like a toy. We might find a malignant lump in our own body one morning. Of course we try to imagine the worst-case scenarios and design contingencies and redundancies. But as the generals say, plans are only good until the first shot in the battle is fired. Then we have to react and adapt, to live in the present tense. We can't change yesterday and have only limited control over tomorrow, but we can do an awful lot about today. We can decide what we will do *right now*—put this book down or keep reading. You can decide how you will live and operate your business for the next next five hours, or how you will conduct your next meeting today. It's like rounding a bend in the river: maybe this is a whitewater day for you. Maybe today's going to be a smooth stretch where you can put the paddle down and be carried along by the current, taking in the scenery. Or you may need to paddle hard to the left, or shoot through a gap to the right, or pull over at a gravel beach. You don't know what the next bend will bring, but you can't control that anyway. If you want to be alive to see it, you need to concentrate on where you are.

We all understand the old distinction between proactive and reactive leadership. We've had it pounded into our heads that we need to be proactive, to get ahead of change and drive outcomes. And that's true. Over and over in this book we've talked about how the successful entrepreneur adapts proactively, cleverly finds solutions, and makes his or her own luck by preparing for opportunity or crisis.

Proactive leadership is praiseworthy, but reactive leadership is often required and realistic. Great entrepreneurs have to have great reflexes because in startups so many things will come at you so quickly. They don't have the luxury of extended history and long business cycles. In the adaptability chapter we said that entrepreneurs don't bend, they evolve. But sometimes those adaptations have to happen in real time, dictated by events. Being nimble means being able to change quickly, to be agile, able to make adjustments on the fly. It's being able to bob and weave, juke and move, serve and volley.

As many have pointed out, ten percent of success comes from what happens to you and ninety percent from how you react to it. Sometimes you have the luxury to reflect and react deliberately. Whenever you can, you should do that. I learned the hard way never to react to a challenging email or submit a proposal until I've thought it through, and I've left plenty of both sitting in a draft folder for many days until I was ready to send, edit, or delete them. But when you don't have that luxury, when you have to think on your feet, it helps to have a nimble mind. Entrepreneurs who want to succeed need to cultivate that capacity.

O IS FOR OPPORTUNISTIC

From the beginning, everything about the Lewis and Clark expedition was the best kind of opportunism. Thomas Jefferson famously opposed Alexander Hamilton's notion of a strong federal government, but when Napoleon needed cash for his wars and put half a continent on sale for $15 million, Jefferson made an exception to his limited government principles and snatched it up. The two men he picked to lead the "Corps of Discovery" had both made use of the opportunities the new nation created. Meriwether Lewis was a bright young man that had come to Jefferson's attention. The president gave him all sorts of important odd jobs, including delivering the State of the Union address to Congress when Jefferson couldn't make it. When the opportunity came to explore the continent westward to the Pacific, he turned to his young go-to guy. Lewis picked an old army buddy, William Clark, who had made a name for himself fighting Indians and opening territories east of the Appalachians. They headed west up the Missouri River without a clear plan for where they were going. They managed to discover some friendly Indians who kept them alive that first winter in the northern plains, and they escaped some of the Sioux tribes who attacked them. In fact, throughout their journey they managed to spot and seize opportunities whenever they presented themselves.

The greatest opportunity came to them in the form of a teenaged girl, Sacagawea. She had been kidnapped as a child from a tribe on the western side of the Rockies and had been brought to live among some of the Plains tribes, where she encountered French fur traders. Since she had a facility with languages, she spoke several tribal tongues as well as French. Lewis and Clark practically stumbled upon this woman and recruited her as their guide and interpreter as they went west. She saved them time af-

is for
OPPORTUNISTIC

ter time by helping them communicate and understand the geography.

Everything about the Lewis and Clark expedition was a lesson in spotting and seizing opportunity. And that's why it should be a great inspiration for entrepreneurs, who must be ready to realize and react to possibilities as they present themselves.

Alright, everyone knows you have to seize opportunity. So what, right? Well, it's not as obvious as it sounds. Too many wannabe entrepreneurs are driven by pure ambition—their vision of what they want to do and be. But ambition can blind us to opportunity. Ambitions are the supply side of life's economy: they are what we want to give to (or in some cases, push upon) the world. Opportunities are what the world wants or needs from us.

Supply-side creativity is a magical thing, beautiful to watch. A great inventor imagines some wonderful new thing and delivers it to the world like Prometheus bringing fire to mankind in Greek mythology. Steve Jobs of Apple and Jeff Bezos of Amazon are recent models of this ideal.

But most successful people are demand-driven, including most of the great inventors and innovators. They see the wants and needs around them, listen to what people are asking for, and figure out how to make and deliver it.

True entrepreneurs have an uncanny instinct for finding and figuring out opportunities. They see gaps and shortcomings, the frustrations or unfilled expectations of people or businesses. Read a book on the history of invention and you'll realize that many of the greatest products and companies in history were not conceived of by someone accidentally spilling a beaker in a lab and discovering some new Wonder Thing. Instead, someone was trying to solve a problem that everyone else was already aware of and working on. Often, they went through countless possible solutions that didn't work before they hit on the right combination that did. After that, ambition kicked in as they came up with a plan to sell it into the marketplace.

The entrepreneur does need ambition, but when an opening presents itself he or she runs through it in much the same way that

Lewis and Clark did. If you look at the history of many of the great entrepreneurial businesses, companies that started out in some garage or shop or whatnot, almost never did the founder have any real idea where it would end up. When entrepreneurs look at the environment around them, it's almost like they have some kind of infrared vision, seeing opportunities in a wavelength of light that's invisible to those around them. Others look at a town, marketplace, community, or demographic segment and can only see what they want to do there. Entrepreneurs look at that same place and intuitively grasp the unmet wants, needs, and desires. Their brains immediately shift into calculating how they can meet that need or plug those gaps in the marketplace. From there, the company often develops in ways the founder never anticipated.

If we want to encourage a more entrepreneurial culture in the United States, we have to cultivate or create the conditions in which opportunities arise so that entrepreneurs have a target-rich environment to hunt in. If we're not careful—if our government policies and cultural shifts are in the wrong direction—we'll kill off a lot of great companies before they're born. We'll see innovation die, startups die, businesses die, unemployment go up—a bleaker future. We need to create a land of endless possibilities and surprises, much like the one Lewis and Clark operated in, because the real entrepreneur thrives in a Lewis-and-Clark environment of possibilities, challenges, and dangers. That might feel like an inhospitable environment to some, but it makes room for innovation, creativity, and hard work.

Successful entrepreneurs pay careful attention to what others want and need—and are shrewd, inventive, and hard-working enough to respond. That's how they get ahead. If you want to succeed, focus less on your ambitious vision and become more observant of the opportunities around you. Then be opportunistic enough to do something about it.

P IS FOR PRAGMATIC

You might think that P would be for *passionate*, *persistent*, or *perfectionistic* (a la Steve Jobs). Those are the kind of enthusiastic, idealistic adjectives that float through the startup blog posts I read, and that I hear from speakers at startup conferences and networking events. They make us feel good because they're positively aspirational—who doesn't want to be passionate? Dogged in pursuing excellence? As my pastor friends would say, those words preach: you'll always get "Amens!" from the choir.

There's an old joke about economic systems that illustrates the pragmatic nature of entrepreneurs:

- Feudalism: You have two cows. Your lord takes some of the milk, and all of the cream.
- Communism: You have two cows. The state takes both and gives you some milk.
- Bureaucratic Socialism: You have two cows. The state takes both, shoots one, milks the other, and then throws the milk away.
- Military Dictatorship: You have two cows. The government takes both and shoots you.
- Entrepreneurial Capitalism: You have two cows. You sell one and buy a bull.

But who gets excited about pragmatism? "Do what works, and drop it if it doesn't" isn't exactly the stuff of pep talks. And entrepreneurial coaches can't exactly bottle and sell pragmatism to wannabe entrepreneurs dreaming of getting rich. You can tell dreamers to dial their "passion" up to a full boil (whatever that really means); you can tell them to keep going like the Little Engine that Could when things don't seem to be working; you can tell them to show that they're superior to everyone around them by never settling for second best. But not a lot of people are going to

P
is for
PRAGMATIC

buy a book that tells them to reality-check their passions, to abandon a bad plan if it isn't going to work before it ruins them, and to take the best deal on the table. But here's the truth entrepreneurs need to hear about passion, persistence, and perfectionism:

The Peril of Passion. We're constantly being told that "passion for our work" is a, even *the*, key to success. In truth, passion is only useful as a *predictor* of performance. No one pays anyone to be passionate about their work. In the marketplace, the *product* matters. Passion may make your work more enjoyable, but it doesn't make it more valuable to others. In fact, passion for our work may actually be counterproductive, if it makes us unable to see our product as others see it and leaves us puzzled as to why they aren't as enthusiastic as we are. Are you passionate about food? Great, but that doesn't mean you'll succeed in starting a restaurant. Are you passionate about fashion? Great, but that doesn't mean you'll be able to turn that into a successful line of clothing and chain of shops. Passionate about collaboration, innovation, ideation, and teams? Great, but that doesn't guarantee that you can start a profitable company. Passion might motivate and drive your interest, but producing and selling enough of a good product at a price that turns a profit is how success is measured in the marketplace. Passion might give an entrepreneur insight, but it might also blind him or her to facts. Passion has to be practical, tempered by pragmatism, to drive success in a startup.

The Problem with Persistence. There's a difference between persistence and perseverance. Persistence is a neutral, descriptive term. It means that you tend to continue to do whatever you're doing. You might persist in doing well, or in going the wrong direction. To persist in doing badly is not a virtue. The wise man knows when to quit, not because something is hard, but because it's foolish to continue on. In fact, the wise person quits more quickly than the fool if he's on the wrong path. Why take another step away from where you need to be? Of course, that assumes that you know where you're supposed to be and whether you're going the wrong way (see "K for Keen" and "C for Clever"). Once you realize you're headed in the wrong direction, to keep going is just to get more lost. Successful entrepreneurs fail fast because they figure out that something isn't working and pull the plug instead of wasting more time, money, and opportunity on a bad bet. Flailing away at a losing plan doesn't turn it into a winner.

That's the difference between persistence and perseverance. Persistence is a neutral quality—you might persist in going the right or wrong way—but perseverance is a virtue. It means to endure difficulty, to have courage and strength in the face of hard circumstances, to stand when it would be so easy to run. To persevere isn't to mindlessly continue in the wrong direction, but to see good things through to their end. Knowing when to stand and when to fold your hand is a function of some of the other qualities in this book.

There's a critical intersection between pragmatism and persistence: sometimes, you have to quit by going forward. When you are so far into a mess that you're past the point of no return, the shortest way out is to press on. You know you've made a mistake in judgment that in turn has made a mess that you're mired in, but the most practical thing to do is grit your teeth and see it through until you can clean it up. Knowing you've stumbled into a pile of crap that you can't pull out of, you grit your teeth, hold your nose, and push through. This is pragmatism at its most naked.

The Paradox of Perfection. The paradox of perfection and its intersection with pragmatism are illustrated by the story of a mathematician and an engineer who find themselves magically transported to a vast hall with a beautiful woman at the other end. An ethereal voice tells them that at the top of each hour, with the ringing of the clock's bells, they may advance half the distance to the woman.

The mathematician (a passionate perfectionist) immediately throws up his hands in disgust. "Well, what's the point? At that rate, I'll never get there."

But as the first bell rings, the engineer (a persistent pragmatist) enthusiastically runs halfway across the hall. "Are you crazy?" shouts the mathematician from the starting point, where he has sat down and given up. "Don't you realize that by halving the distance, you'll never get to her?"

"That's OK," shouts back the engineer. "Eventually, I'll get close enough for my purposes!"

Perfection is an abstraction, a mathematical concept unattainable in human endeavors. We can describe a perfect circle, but can we cook a perfect meal, or build a perfect house, or write a perfect novel? Can your house be perfectly clean, or can you raise perfect children, or can you come up with the perfect solution to a problem? Perfectionists often quit too easily because reality can never live up to their standards and they would rather not try than to try and fail. In the real world, perfectionists rarely win. Far too often, they end up being underachievers, because if they can't do something perfectly, they won't do it at all. Winners know when something is good enough.

The pragmatic entrepreneur knows when something is done well enough to let it go and move on to the next challenge. His or her standards are high, but not "perfection," whatever that is. Perfectionists get stuck in a loop of effort and frustration trying to make something perfect. They never turn out perfect work because perfection is unattainable. And because they cannot recognize that what they've done is good enough for their purposes (even though the standards might be very high), they achieve very little. Usually, they get frustrated and walk away from what they are trying to do, or they refuse to try. But they don't let it go; it eats them up inside. They are not often happy people. While the perfectionist miserably stews about the imperfections of the world and his or her inability to fix them, the winners have figured out how to get things done close enough to perfect in order to move on to their next challenge.

If we were to package the three P's often peddled as the keys to entrepreneurial success—passion, persistence, and perfectionism—pragmatism might be considered to be the opposite of that bundle. The pragmatic entrepreneur is concerned with what will actually work to help his or her business succeed. Is that amoral? Uninspiring? Perhaps, but it's grounded in reality. William James said that pragmatism was "the cash value of the truth." For men and women who start businesses, calculating the cash value of the truth might very well be the difference between success and bankruptcy.

Q IS FOR QUALIFIED

Once upon a time, there was a brewer named Duncan. Duncan was a master craftsman: he had learned the art of brewing by serving as an apprentice to his uncle, who had learned it from his father, who had learned it from his father. For generations, the secrets to making the most excellent beer within a hundred miles had been handed down by oral tradition and hands-on training. Duncan didn't think about the proportions of ingredients or the steps in the process, for they had become second nature to him. And his beer was so wonderful that good folks journeyed from the distant corners of the province, over field and stream, to visit his inn and taste his pints. On any given night the place was packed, the patrons toasting Duncan and begging him to start a brewery and share the wonder of his brews throughout the country.

So Duncan did. He borrowed a great deal of money to construct a building and filled it with copper kettles and equipment to bottle his ales. He wasn't sure if the bankers had played straight with him, for Duncan had no experience with finance. But he believed in his vision. He hired brewers and apprentices to work underneath him, and buyers to obtain barley and hops. He had workers to bottle and teamsters to carry it to distant markets in the great cities of the land.

His first efforts were successful. Distant customers loved his product and demanded more. Duncan went back to the bankers and borrowed more money, still unsure if he was getting the better end of the bargain. He hired builders to expand his brewery, but to do so he had to buy adjacent real estate through land agents and deal with tax collectors and the mayor of the town. He was faced with what seemed like a thousand expensive decisions. Meanwhile, some of his new brewers weren't keeping to the methods that had made Duncan's beer so tasty. He had to fire a

Q is for
QUALIFIED

few, retrain others, and watch the rest like a hawk. The bottles he was buying were of inconsistent quality, and many broke in the wagons on the way to market. His workers wanted raises, and the buyers had trouble getting the right kind of hops and barley in the quantities that he needed them, when he needed them.

Duncan had loved brewing beer and the joy it brought to those who drank it. He knew that he was a great brewer, but as his business grew he spent less time in the brewhouse and more in the office. Before he knew it, he wasn't brewing at all, or chatting with happy drinkers. It seemed he was talking to his bankers every week. With all the time he spent on real estate and equipment, buildings and supply chain management, hiring and firing, pricing and transport, Duncan hadn't brewed a beer in years, but he needed one every day.

Sometimes, on late nights when he was poring over papers in his office instead of pouring pints in his pub, he would admit to himself that he wasn't happy. He didn't like being a businessman. He didn't have the right tools for the job. He missed being a brewer. That's what he had been best at.

This is the Craftsman's Dilemma. The craftsman has to be competent or qualified enough to start the business, to understand it enough to create the initial product or service, launch the business, sell and deliver the first batches, and to hire and manage the first employees. But if he or she is good enough to get past that point, a new set of skills is required. Eventually, the skill demanded isn't brewing the beer—it's brewing the company that brews the beer. Just because the craftsman could make "the thing" doesn't mean he can make the thing that makes the thing. The craftsman doesn't necessarily grow into the entrepreneur.

The dilemma is that the craftsman has to be qualified enough in making the thing to lead and supervise the company, but the critical skill, the primary qualification, for leading and supervising the company is entrepreneurship. But if entrepreneurs forget the craft that built the company, they run the risk of alienating the craftsmen who work under them, losing quality control, or no longer understanding what customers want or how to compete with new and improved products.

Michael Gerber's game-changing book *The eMyth* helped us all to understand that the entrepreneur has to work *on* the business, not *in* the business. But the Craftsman's Dilemma is the paradox that the entrepreneur can't work on the business unless he or she works in the business enough to be qualified to lead.

How qualified? Business history is full of examples of executives brought in under the premise that "the thing" (the product) is just an interchangeable widget. Famously, Steve Jobs was replaced at Apple in the 1980s by John Sculley, who had been the CEO of Pepsi. The board of Apple reasoned that leadership skills were interchangeable and that the competencies required didn't include craftsmanship of the product. They figured that if Sculley could build a company that made soda pop, he could build a company that made computers. That proved disastrously wrong. Steve Jobs ultimate skill was entrepreneurship—of Apple (it's not clear he could have started a soft drink company or construction firm). He was competent and qualified enough in the thing that Apple made (computers) to build Apple into one of the world's greatest companies. For a while in his career it didn't look like he could rise above the Craftsman Dilemma, but ultimately he did. It wasn't easy, and most craftsmen never find the right balance.

That's because the transition from craftsman to entrepreneur to CEO isn't a one-time step function, a single leap. There are stages of organizational development, and each one tests different skills. The entrepreneur needs to grow and develop to make the move from each level to the next: starting with the first handful of employees who all report directly to the entrepreneur, growing until there are a few dozen employees, forcing the entrepreneur to manage through layers, and so on until the startup becomes an enterprise requiring enterprise-level leadership skills. The bigger the company, the more the entrepreneur deals with financing and legal issues, and the more disconnected he or she gets from the craft that started the business. This is the source of endless complaining by workers and consumers, because the CEO seems to no longer understand the underlying product or service that the brand is built on. Always, the entrepreneur has to be qualified and experienced enough in making the thing to lead others to make the thing.

Leadership plateaus occur when entrepreneurs like Duncan the brewer get stuck because they've gotten too far away from the craft and aren't qualified to meet the demands of the growing enterprise. Some learn and solve the problem and move on—and some don't. Some founding entrepreneurs are willing to hand off the reigns to others who are more capable of taking the company to the next level, preferring to stay in their comfort zone (like the co-founder of Apple, Steve Wozniak). There are business owners who start companies and sell when it gets too big for them, and there are some who don't but should. It can be painful for everyone concerned when founders sell the company because it's gone beyond their craftsmanship and they don't have the entrepreneurial talent to grow with it. It's an old story that's happened uncountable times: a magical startup gets too big, the founders start to fumble and stumble, they sell, an "expert" CEO is brought in from a bigger industry competitor, and the magic is lost.

If you're a craftsman like Duncan, you might be considering starting a company. If you go forward, do so knowing that you will have to grow in the entrepreneurial arts. That's probably going to be painful. But never lose sight, or connection, with the craftsmanship that got you started or the product that your business is built on. That's a tension you'll need to manage.

R
is for
RESPONSIBLE

R IS FOR RESPONSIBLE

A contradiction is a pair of things that cannot both be true at the same time (the rug on my studio floor can't be both square *and* circular). A paradox is a pair of ideas that *can* both be true, but feel like they shouldn't be because there's a conceptual tension between them. There is a paradox at the heart of entrepreneurship: the great thing about being your own boss is that you get to be your own boss, but the terrible thing about being your own boss is that you *have* to be your own boss.

Many would-be entrepreneurs hope that owning their own business will finally set them free. They aspire to the right of self-determination. They long to control their own destinies and schedules. For certain personalities, this dream of self-actualization is so intoxicating that they leave lucrative jobs, wagering their family fortunes to pursue it. But too many get to the end of the rainbow only to discover that the pot of gold is heavy. True, they aren't responsible to bosses over them, but they are responsible for the people under them and the business they've created. They can set their calendars and to-do lists as they see fit, but they are solely responsible for the consequences of those choices. They can head into the workplace at dawn or noon, they can leave early or stay late, they can hire or fire people, green-light or red-light projects, paint the walls purple or buy everyone pizza for lunch. *Finally,* they rejoice, *there is no one telling me "No!"* But every choice is a brick that goes into baggage that only the owner can carry. The choices accumulate, box them in, impinge on the very freedom they set out to find. The entrepreneur is never again as free as he or she was on the first hour of the first morning they decided to start their business. After that, every decision leads to other decisions and builds walls that form rooms full of clutter and stories and obligation, and the entrepreneur has to live inside them. The choice to name your business X means that it can't be Y; every piece of equipment bought is a bill to pay, every hour spent here isn't spent there, every employee hired is another mouth to feed out of overhead, every employee fired creates work that won't get done.

The paradox of entrepreneurship is the tension between idealistic liberty and the reality of responsibilities. It's why so many people who start businesses because they were enchanted by the dream quickly feel trapped inside of it. They get to keep what they build, but they have to live within it. That's why R is for responsible: all entrepreneurs are responsible for what they create, but successful ones can embrace that burden. True entrepreneurs don't feel like their dreams pulled a bait-and-switch on them. Wannabe and poseur entrepreneurs chafe under the obligations. Real entrepreneurs wear their choices like a hand-tailored suit: they are comfortable with the fit, and it flatters them. It's the secret to their success.

I'm no psychologist, but I have a theory that a particular mental trait is essential for successful entrepreneurs. It has to do with the idea of "locus of control." Locus of control is the mental sense each of us has about what is driving our life and what accounts for the state of the world around us. Our sense of the locus of control isn't conscious, and it may not even be controllable. I think it's baked into our cake by the time we're out of childhood. It becomes part of our brain's operating system, a product of nature and nurture (but probably mostly nature). Some of us sense the locus of control externally, believing that what happens to us is primarily driven by outside forces and other people. These people never really own their failures—which in their mind are always someone or something else's fault. Some of these folks might be attracted to the idea of starting their own business because freedom is a beautiful dream, but they will probably never succeed because they can't own their outcomes. I think that if there were some way to test it, we'd find that successful entrepreneurs have an internal locus of control. They perceive that their world, for better or worse, is basically shaped by their own choices or responses to events.

They're not only willing to own the outcomes of their efforts, but they couldn't imagine not doing so.

If this is a baked-in personality trait, then you can't shift your locus of control any more than you can switch from being an introvert to an extrovert. But just as an introvert can learn to be polite and work with people, and an extrovert can learn to be alone long enough to accomplish tasks, so we can learn to accept responsibility. In fact, the purpose of child-rearing and education used to be to help children to grow up in just this way. Being a grown up is hard, and as a nation we're hard at work helping people to avoid it by constructing a culture of immaturity and dependence. But as Margaret Thatcher once said, the facts of life are conservative: in the end, consequences catch up with us. Refusing to grow up is only delaying the inevitable.

Growing to accept consequences is perhaps the central theme of *The Rime of the Ancient Mariner,* an epic poem by Samuel Taylor Coleridge. It tells of a voyage during the Age of Discovery, led by a hard and harsh sea captain. Somewhere in the great Southern Ocean, the ship finds the "doldrums," a great expanse of flat, windless sea. The ship cannot move, and stores of food and water run out. The crew is dying of thirst in an ocean, which the narrator laments in a famous line: "Water, water everywhere, nor any drop to drink." The captain sees an albatross, considered an omen of good luck by sailors of that age. But he blames the albatross for their mishap, and he shoots it with his crossbow. It falls onto the deck. The dying crew stares at it, knowing they are doomed because the captain has shot the one thing they hoped would save them. They hang the bird around his neck. It is a weight, a decaying reminder that he is responsible for their fate. That is how the phrase "an albatross around the neck" became a metaphor for having to bear heavy consequences for one's actions.

The paradox of entrepreneurship is really just the paradox of becoming a grownup. Being young is fun because the future is nothing but possibilities. When I was nineteen years old, sitting in a student pub drinking beer with my other creative friends (the drinking age for beer in Colorado was eighteen at the time, so the student center in Boulder had a pub that was *rather* popular), I conceived the dream of someday owning my own creative studio. My buddies would go in on it with me as partners. It was a half-baked idea and had a stupid name (we were going to call it "EarthPower Productions," from a science fiction/fantasy book that we had all read and loved). Of course, we imagined ourselves becoming hugely successful by developing movie and book projects. We had absolutely no clue what we were talking about, what the industry was like, how to get there, or how exactly it would all work. Sitting in that student pub at the University of Colorado, all I could imagine was that someday I would wake up in my cool house and drive my cool car to some cool studio with wood floors and exposed bricks in some cool downtown, and my partners and I would sit around and come up with cool ideas for books and films. We'd have a lot of fun making a lot of money. I didn't know how any of this could actually happen, I just aspired to a lifestyle that was free and creative, in which I would be responsible to no one but myself.

Well, life took a lot of twists and turns. But when I was in my early forties I finally got around to starting a creative company. It wasn't anything like what I thought it would be like. It's really hard, and we don't always get it right—in fact, I make a ton of mistakes. The industry is crowded and competitive. Sometimes clients are difficult and opportunities evaporate. Things you want to do don't turn out. The choices that you made when you were nineteen and twenty-four and thirty-six and forty-one all begin to compound. You can't undo them or shake them off. They become albatrosses dangling around your neck, things that you have to carry. As I write this book, I do have a studio with wood floors and exposed brick in a downtown area, but it's nothing like what I imagined sitting in that pub in the student center in Boulder—absolutely nothing. I'm willing to take responsibility for all my choices, but that responsibility sometimes seems less a privilege and more like... well, like being a grownup.

My story isn't unique; doctors and homebuilders and software developers and folks who own manufacturing companies might tell similar stories about coming to terms with the reality of their dreams. Growing up means accepting responsibility, and at a minimum entrepreneurs must be willing to be grownups.

S is for
SUCCESSFUL

S IS FOR SUCCESSFUL

These two words aren't necessarily the most important in this book, but they're pretty important. They go to the heart of why some entrepreneurs succeed and some don't. They might seem silly to some of you, and they'll feel insulting or insensitive to others. But your reaction to them is a sort of Rorschach Test that reveals more about you than it does about me, and it probably gives some strong indication as to whether you're cut out for the startup game. Ready? Here they are:

Winners win.

Well, obviously, right? But look deeper. It's not just a circular definition or a tautology. It's a recognition that the defining characteristic of successful people is that they actualize possibilities for success. They have the capacity to come out on top, and they carry that through to completion. They can get it done, and they do. They have a knack, a touch, an edge, a certain something that comes out in competition and helps them beat the best that others bring into the arena. But how do you define or articulate or identify this quality before the game begins, other than standing back and letting it play out until the winner emerges?

In 1961, the Soviet Union was the first country to put a man into orbit in a deadly-serious global competition called the Space Race. One nation, either the USA or the USSR, would dominate this high frontier, and they both threw everything they had at it. President John F. Kennedy promised that by the end of the decade, the United States would put a man on the moon, which were bold words when we were already losing. Tom Wolfe's classic book *The Right Stuff*, and the movie made from it, capture the manic way that the United States threw its prestige and treasure into this race.

The newly-formed agency called NASA went in search of men who could be the first astronauts, who could carry the hopes, fears, and pride of a nation. But what kind of men? They had to be best of the best, able to meet the physical, mental, technical, and emotional demands of leading America to the moon. Where would you find them? They looked at the best fighter pilots in the military, who also had advanced engineering educations, athleticism and endurance, mental and emotional resilience. They had to be articulate, handsome, and wholesome role models. What would you call the right combination of all these attributes? What they were looking for was intangible, elusive. It was easy to spot people who were *wrong* for the job, but when you narrowed your pool down to the top one percent of the top one per cent of the top one per cent of the population, and all the candidates met all the formal criteria, then what? The NASA people began calling it "the Right Stuff." They found a handful, the Mercury Seven astronauts, who had the Right Stuff.

The thing about the Right Stuff is that you either have it or you don't. Whether it's astronauts or championship athletes, some people will rise to the occasion, dominate, and win. They will land a malfunctioning Lunar Command Module in the dust a quarter of a million miles from home, or sink the come-from-behind jump shot at the buzzer to win the World Championship. The Right Stuff can't be measured or check-listed, but it emerges. It is proven in the pressure of the arena. Winners win.

At conferences and networking events I meet people who introduce themselves as entrepreneurs because they start a lot of little companies. But entrepreneurs aren't just people who start things—anybody can start stuff. Entrepreneurs start businesses that survive. Successful entrepreneurs start businesses that succeed. They win.

Let's be totally clear about one thing, though: they don't necessarily win at everything in life. Their marriage might be a mess, their kids might hate them, and they might not have any genuine friends. They might have big egos and bank accounts, but small souls and shrunken little hearts. In the end, success in business is only of value for this life. As Jesus said, what does it profit a man to gain the whole world and lose his own soul? But when it comes to starting and running a business, think twice before you step into the arena and compete against these winners.

On the other hand, people who have rarely won anything, who don't like competition, and who are turned off by alpha males and females might want to think twice before going all in on starting a business. While successful entrepreneurs don't succeed at everything, I guarantee you that they've won before. Winning is a habit, which is why I get concerned when people say things like, "It doesn't matter whether we win or lose, just how we play the game," or, "We learn more from losing from winning." Sure, an occasional loss is instructive, even healthy and helpful, if you can debrief how it happened and apply that understanding to the next game. But losing too much just teaches you how to lose. Winning teaches you how to win. Successful entrepreneurs have won enough to know how to do it, to get used to winning, to gain confidence and competence at it. They know how to pull it off when it counts.

There's a great action movie that came out in 1996 called *The Rock*, starring Sean Connery and Nicolas Cage. Terrorists have taken over the old prison on Alcatraz Island and placed missiles with nerve gas on it, pointed across the bay at San Francisco. Cage is a scientist who knows how to defuse the missiles, and Connery is an old special forces guy who had once been imprisoned on Alcatraz and had found a way to escape, so he's inserted with Cage and a team of Navy SEALs to find the launchers. Well, the SEAL team is ambushed by the terrorists and wiped out, leaving only Cage and Connery to save the day. Cage is a lab guy, and he's not used to gunplay, skulking around in tunnels, and all this violence. In a critical scene in the sewers under the prison, he's terrified and ready to quit, to sneak back out to safety. Connery gives him this little speech, more or less saying, "We have to go forward, the clock is running down to launch and millions of people are going to die." Cage tries to straighten himself and "man up." He swallows and says, "Alright, I'll do my best." Connery cuts him off with a sharp "No!" and delivers this line the way only Sean Connery could: "Losers whine about doing their best; winners go home and [make love to] the prom queen."

While some are spinning off endless startups that sputter and die or struggle along doing their best, successful entrepreneurs, the ones with the Right Stuff, win. Because that's what winners do.

Do you have the Right Stuff? Only you know, and only results will prove it one way or the other. But I know how to tell if you have the Wrong Stuff: if you're not playing to win, you might as well fold and go home.

T IS FOR TEACHABLE

I'm concerned that some readers might get the impression that I think the entrepreneurial personality is headstrong, a potent mix of nothing but cunning intuition and decisive pragmatism. Clearly, those are only part of the total package. It's more likely that some readers will cherry-pick the chapters of this book, finding reinforcement for their particular self-image. If they fancy themselves as bold visionaries, they'll focus on "B is for Brave" and ignore "R is for Responsible." None of the twenty-six qualities exist in isolation, but form an integrated character in the entrepreneur. *Judgmental* is tempered by *keen*, *opportunistic* by *pragmatic*, *frugal* by *brave*. Unsuccessful entrepreneurs have unbalanced personalities, emphasizing some of these to the exclusion of others.

That's why I want to stress teachability. The dictionary defines teachability as the ability to learn by instruction. The "by instruction" part is important. Almost every animal can learn. Block a line of ants and they'll figure out how to get around the barrier, or hang a bird feeder and watch the squirrels find a way to climb down the rope to get at the seeds. Some people only learn by painful experience, by burning themselves on hot stoves and smashing their thumbs with hammers so many times that it finally dawns on them to do things differently. Weirdly, some are proud of learning everything the hard way, bragging that they graduated from the School of Hard Knocks.

I'd much rather learn by instruction than screwing up and paying the tuition on the back end through painful consequences. I haven't always, but if I could have I would have. I've always told my children that I wanted them to be smarter and more successful than me, unapologetically offering them advice and giving them worthwhile educational opportunities. If they could avoid

T is for
TEACHABLE

the years, money, and opportunities I wasted by learning through instruction instead, I prayed that they would. How much easier it would have been for all of us, and how much further along we would be now, if we had listened and learned when parents, teachers, mentors, books, etc. tried to teach us things they knew we needed to know? Aldous Huxley argued that "experience only teaches the teachable," meaning that painful experiences may not make some entrepreneurs *wiser* business leaders, but merely help them avoid pain or getting caught.

Entrepreneurs need to be teachable because they don't have time to learn everything by trial and error. Don't get me wrong, their biographies are full of lessons learned the hard way. But every one of those lessons is a lost day, a lost dollar, a lost opportunity. The School of Hard Knocks is expensive and shouldn't be romanticized. Shrewd entrepreneurs learn everything that will give them an edge from wherever they can learn it, as cheaply and quickly as possible—school, books, websites, conferences, consultants, coaches, mentors, whatever. If the entrepreneur is teachable, some of their best teachers are customers, colleagues, and competitors. Bill Gates, one of the most successful entrepreneurs of all time, said, "Your most unhappy customers are your greatest source of learning." They will tell you what they don't like, what you're doing wrong, what isn't working. A teachable entrepreneur channels this feedback into productive change and turns potential losses into wins. Entrepreneurs with unteachable and stubborn spirits double down on their mistakes. That's when they become stupid, as opposed to merely ignorant. Ignorance is not knowing something, and there's no shame in it if you acknowledge it and learn. If you don't know, ask—most people will be happy to inform you. Refusing to learn, being incapable of being taught, is stupidity. That's almost never forgiven by anyone, and in the marketplace of startups it is almost never without consequences.

As we've seen throughout this book, entrepreneurs are unique people with many impressive qualities. They are clever and successful, keen and decisive; they adapt and grasp opportunities. For all these reasons, they are prone to being know-it-alls.

Humble people never think they are the smartest person in the room, but a successful entrepreneur might actually *be* the smartest person in the room. But teachable entrepreneurs know that if that's true, then they're hanging around the wrong rooms. It doesn't help to be around people that can't teach you anything. Teachable entrepreneurs will go out of their way to get in rooms full of people smarter than them. If the ego can be tamed, knowledge can expand and the mind can grow. We don't learn much in echo chambers that only praise our ideas, reinforce our thinking, or confirm our prejudices. That's why the Internet isn't always a good teacher: it's too easy to click away from opinions we disagree with. The genuinely teachable entrepreneur will seek out challenging relationships that force him or her to grow. He or she will forge alliances, make unusual friendships, attend conferences, and correspond with people who know more about certain subjects. They make a habit of learning as much as possible from any source that gives them an edge in innovating, analyzing, or managing their businesses.

Teachability doesn't just mean being around people or sources that stimulate; it means the entrepreneur tries new things so they can always be learning something. Doing the same old things the way they've always been done before is impossible for entrepreneurial personalities. Successful entrepreneurs love to learn because by definition they start new businesses and create new products, and that takes constant learning. Even in their non-business lives, most successful entrepreneurs are always learning something: playing a new sport, taking up a new hobby, traveling to new places, or exploring new ideas. Many of them like to tinker and play with technology. They need the challenges. They are willing to be a beginner at something so they have another challenge to chew on. Meister Eckhart, a medieval German philosopher, said, "Be willing to be a beginner every single morning." In other words, put yourself in situations where you can learn and grow.

Teachability is not a skill, it's a character trait, and I think our character is largely set by the time we're about six or seven years old. After that, we're adapting our character to our environment. If you resisted and resented learning as a child, you'll chafe at it for the rest of your life. If that's you, then it's going to be a hurdle in your entrepreneurial career. You'll stubbornly refuse to acknowledge your ignorance and insist on learning everything the hard way. While you flail away, bushwhacking through the forest, competitors with more open minds and teachable characters will have bought a trail map and gotten there first.

A teachable entrepreneur knows how and when to listen. That's also baked into their character when they are children. Some kids refuse to listen to anyone who challenges their will, much less who gives them instruction. As they grow, they become defensive and ignore or shut down opposing voices. They surround themselves with sycophants and yes-men. They read and believe their own press clippings. They can't hear any voice that tells them they might be wrong, so they are vulnerable to being *proved* wrong in the marketplace by competitors who can listen and learn from others.

Life is full of teachable moments, opportunities for learning and growth. Many of these are painful, but they don't have to be. Many of my most teachable moments were disasters that forced me to learn while I licked my wounds—but not all my most enduring lessons were like that. Many were classroom lectures by gifted teachers that have stuck with me for thirty years, life-changing ideas highlighted in the pages of beloved books I read, insights and epiphanies I gained at conferences or retreats, wisdom spoken into my life by friends or mentors, a revolutionary technique I discovered while surfing the web, even tricks or "hacks" some expert taught me. The successful entrepreneur doesn't run in ruts or have a lazy mind. Successful entrepreneurs search for these teachable moments, because they have learned (often the hard way) that instruction has often been the key to their success.

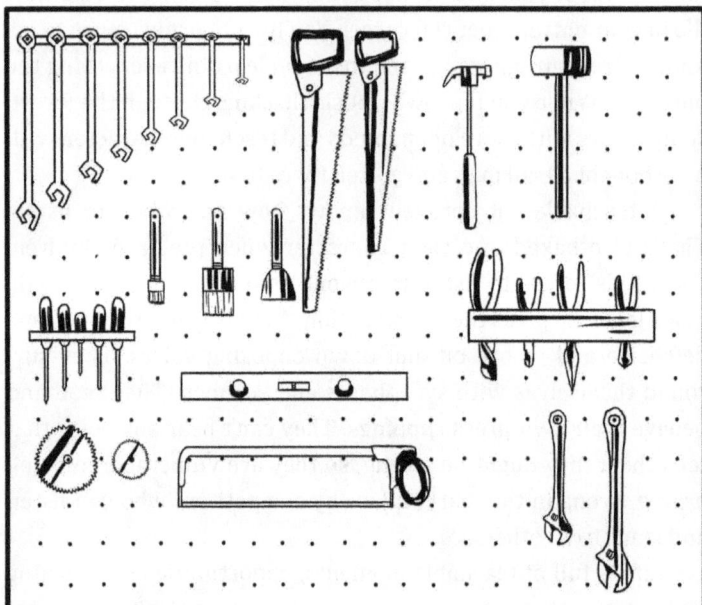

U is for
USEFUL

U IS FOR USEFUL

The ancient Greek philosopher Aristotle said that the greatest virtues (positive qualities) a man can possess are those that are most useful to other people. Now, far be it from me to edit Aristotle, but I'm not sure that he was completely right. Some things are good just because they're intrinsically good, not because they are useful to others. But I think he was spot-on when it comes to entrepreneurship: entrepreneurs are at their best when they are being useful. The qualities in this book reach their highest form when applied in ways that are of practical help to those around them: customers, colleagues, vendors, or the business as a whole. Their success is ultimately meaningless unless it benefits their family, shareholders, employees, society, and the world. They must learn to play well with others, contribute to every team, and add value to every transaction. If we imagine sets of business, personal, and people skills as toolboxes, they need to have lots of tools in those toolboxes. And they need to know how to pull the right tools out and use them at the right times in the right ways to make a difference for those around them.

I remember taking a final exam in graduate school. The class had studied different approaches to leadership and management, and one of the essay questions on the final was weirdly simple: "What is the most effective leadership style?"

It felt like a setup to me—and it was. The professor was trying to get us to pick one leadership/management style so he could pigeonhole or classify us (this guy is "dominant and directive," she's "data-driven and dispassionate," he's "collaborative and collegial," she's "serving and supportive," etc.). This professor definitely had a favorite—there *was* a right answer if you wanted an A from him.

I thought for a moment, and then I wrote something like this:

I object to the premise of this question, that there is a best way to lead an organization. It's like asking, "Which is the best golf club?" The right leadership style is the one that best suits the needs and particulars of the situation. In a round of golf you have fourteen clubs in your bag, from putter to driver. Which is the "best" one? Well, that depends on a lot of variables. How far away from the hole are you? Is the shot uphill or downhill? How thick is the grass? Are you lying on grass, or in the sand, or on the green? Is there wind? From which direction? How are your skills? Which clubs have you been hitting well in practice lately? What's your score at that point in the round, and how much risk can you tolerate on this shot? The best club is the one that best answers all of these questions. Saying that there is a best club or that you have a favorite is like saying that you like the sand wedge so much that you use it on every shot, regardless of the variables. A good leader should be able to apply the style most useful to the situation.

The professor hated my response and gave me no points for failing to answer the question. But to this day, I'm sure I was right and he was wrong. As I got to know him and learned about his own career, I realized that he was like a guy who uses his sand wedge on every shot—which, in my humble opinion, is why he was a professor and not a successful entrepreneur. Entrepreneurs have to be able to hit with all the clubs in their bag and to use all the tools in their toolbox, depending on where they are and what they're facing. If they can't learn to be useful to their customers, they won't have any. If they won't be useful to their colleagues and employees, their company will drift. If they can't be useful to the business, they become the anchor holding it back.

It is crucial for the entrepreneur to have strategic, critical, and introspective thinking skills. But, as Aristotle said, the highest form of entrepreneurial thinking is to apply them in useful ways. It does you no good in a startup to form strategic plans, poke holes in bad ideas, or reflect on who you are if you can't be of practical help when it's needed. We need to learn to think bigger, but act smaller. That means that if our minds are full of little thoughts, little hurts, little ambitions, and little rivalries, we become little people. We need to think big: see the larger picture, get plugged into the larger world around us, follow big ideas, and cast big visions. But big thinking can lead to big problems: grandiosity, arrogance, and elitism. Don't become so enamored with the forest that you can't see the trees, much less accomplish anything of practical value. Think at the 30,000-foot strategic level, but act practically and specifically, getting stuff done on the ground. Dreamers and idealists are great, but the best dreamers are the ones who can turn their dreams into practical realities that add value to everyone around them.

Usefulness is at the heart of entrepreneurship, on all sides of your business model. If you aren't useful to your customers, you don't have a business. If your employees aren't useful to you, why are they employees? If you aren't useful to your employees beyond giving them a paycheck, you'll just get a paycheck's worth of work out of them. An entrepreneur has to have a practical eye and a nose for what is and isn't useful in all transactions. Those instincts help him or her know what to make and how to price and sell it, to figure out who to hire or fire, which buildings to rent or which supplies to buy, and how to spend time and money.

A useful entrepreneur can build teams that collaborate productively because he or she brings something valuable to the table that sets the trajectory for a project. Good entrepreneurs know when they are adding value to the equation and invest time there. They also recognize when they're just taking up space in a meeting or on a team and either adjust their contribution or spend their time somewhere else where they can add value. As a matter of fact, a valuable entrepreneur knows that adding value doesn't always mean cheerleading or chipping in just to participate. Sometimes, the most useful contribution a business owner can make to a team is to tell it that it's on the wrong track. Pope Francis said, "I like it when someone tells me, 'I don't agree.' This is a true collaborator. When they say, 'Oh, how great, how great, how great,' that's not useful." Sometimes, the most useful thing an owner can contribute to a team is to pull the plug on a project or person that is going the wrong direction before more time and money is wasted. The great American architect Frank Lloyd Wright said that, "An architect's most useful tools are an eraser at the drafting board, and a wrecking bar at the site."

Are you useful to those around you? Do you add value to transactions, teams, and meetings? If not, you need to add some tools to your toolbox or some clubs to your bag and teach yourself how and when to use them. It begins with an honest assessment. What valuable skills do you actually have, and have proven proficiency with in practical situations? All entrepreneurs should be developing their existing skills and working to acquire new ones. Successful entrepreneurs never take their abilities for granted, but practice and sharpen them all the time. They never know when they might come in handy.

V IS FOR VIGILANT

When I lived in California, a friend of mine who was a policeman in Los Angeles used to come over to our house for dinner every couple of weeks. I always looked forward to his visits because he'd tell us about crimes and cases he was working on. His work stories were a lot more interesting than mine.

One evening, we watched a movie about a criminal mastermind being tracked down by a clever detective, and he went off on a rant about how the movies portrayed criminals as shrewd and sophisticated. In his experience, most of them became criminals precisely because they *weren't* shrewd or sophisticated, and it didn't take too much detective work to figure out "who done it." He gave us some examples, including this one.

One day, he got a call about a bank robbery. When he arrived at the scene, the uniformed cops were interviewing witnesses. Everyone reported that the robber was of average height and weight and wore blue jeans—there was nothing distinguishing about the guy. He wore a long-sleeved shirt and ski mask, so nobody had seen his face. The other cops had waited for my friend to arrive so he could interview the teller.

He sat down with her. She said the guy came up to her window, handed her a note saying that he had a gun in his pocket, and demanded money. Bank policy was to hand it over so no one got hurt, so she did. My friend asked all the obvious questions. Height and weight? Average. Unusual accent? None. Tattoos? None visible. Limps or lisps or missing limbs? None. My friend sighed as he wound up the interview. Could she think of any additional information that might help the police to apprehend the robber?

"Well," she said, "I have his name, address, and phone number. Will that help?"

"What? Why didn't you tell us that before?"

V is for
VIGILANT

"No one asked."

The teller explained that the guy had first come into the bank in street clothes with no mask. He waited in line, and when he got to the teller's window he handed her one of his own personal checks, written to cash—essentially, he had tried to withdraw money from his own account. The teller checked his balance and told him that she was sorry, but he was overdrawn and she couldn't cash the check. The man looked frustrated and agitated. Clearly, he needed the money and had counted on being able to withdraw it. He left the check on the counter, walked back out to his car and sat in it, looking distressed. She could see him through the window. Evidently, he was forming his Criminal Mastermind Plan. After about ten minutes he got out of the car, but now he had pulled on a ski mask. He came back up to the same teller and handed her the note. She put the money in the bag, and he went back out and drove away.

She handed the check to the cop. Sure enough, printed on it was the guy's name, address, and phone number. In what can only be described as clever detective work, my friend drove over to the guy's apartment and knocked. The robber opened the door, and my friend saw the money stacked on the coffee table behind him.

It wasn't exactly shouting, "Colonel Mustard in the conservatory with the candlestick!" But the case was closed.

What's this got to do with entrepreneurship? From the day the entrepreneur opens his business, he needs to be on guard against costly mistakes, incompetence, deception, and outright fraud. In an ideal world, the entrepreneur shouldn't have to do all this. But in case you haven't been paying attention to current events, it's not an ideal world. Given the human condition, entrepreneurs must be vigilant. Vendors, employees, partners, customers, competitors, or government inspectors won't always be diligent, honest, accurate, or trustworthy. An entrepreneur who takes everything for granted and everyone at their word might be good hearted, but he or she is almost certainly shortsighted. Business owners need healthy skepticism and active vigilance because their business is their family's livelihood. Losses come out of their pocket and sometimes add to their already heavy debt.

Vigilance is defined as "keeping careful watch for possible danger or difficulties." Synonyms include *watchful, observant, attentive,* and *alert.* It comes from the Latin word *vigilante,* meaning "keeping awake." A vigil is a period of purposeful wakefulness during the night, especially to keep watch or pray. Entrepreneurs need to be vigilant, staying awake, alert, and attentive to external and internal threats to the health and profitability of their business.

What sorts of things does the entrepreneur need to be watching for? Outside of the business, there are a thousand threats that can't be taken lightly. Inside the business, the owner needs to stay awake and aware of any number of problems that can creep into his or her workforce.

1. **Employee incompetence or malfeasance.** The owner needs to not only watch for employees who are criminally dishonest, but also those who aren't effective because of a range of shortcomings, including laziness, bad attitudes, incompetence, and negligence. How do you spot poor performance early and address it? There are plenty of resources and consultants that can help, but this isn't a chapter about HR or performance management. This is about the quality of the entrepreneur: is he or she willing to be vigilant enough to prevent slippage and fix the problems? Entrepreneurs sometimes hesitate to hold employees accountable. In the early days they need people. Desperate for help, they sometimes let things slip in order to keep the startup crew onboard. They haven't yet established processes, procedures, and standards. They let the first batch of pioneering employees set those standards and rules, and lose control. Startups sometimes can't pay as much as established competitors and are under enormous pressure, so they let things slide. The entrepreneur is so busy innovating, selling, and developing, that he or

she doesn't have time to manage and sometimes overestimates how committed the pioneer generation of employees are to the company vision, or to the entrepreneur.

2. **Employees that can't go to the next level.** Some employees are "Peter Principled," meaning that they've risen as far as they are capable of going—actually, they've gone further than they should have and are in over their heads. Without dramatic retooling, such an employee is going to hold the company back, not help it move forward. This is especially painful when it's an employee who played a crucial role in the birth or early development of the business. Entrepreneurs sometimes let sympathy and loyalty (which are *not* bad qualities) lead them to ignore these limitations. Cutting off someone who helped you get this far feels like betrayal. The employee will see it that way, and lots of people around them will as well. That's why the capacity to make these decisions is one of the essential traits of the successful entrepreneur.

Spotting and solving these problems won't always be as easy as the "Case of the Bank Robber's Bounced Check." Vigilance means being alert and seeing what's hard to see, sometimes because it's so obvious that we become oblivious to it. It reminds me of another story, this one about a large building project in Moscow during the Soviet era. There were all sorts of valuable materials stacked around the job site, and to keep the local workers from stealing them, guards searched them as they left at the end of the day. For many days, the same worker would stand in the inspection line at quitting time, pushing a wheelbarrow loaded with straw. The guard was suspicious, and every day he searched the straw carefully. Sometimes he made the worker empty the straw onto the ground and sift through it. He even had the straw analyzed by a lab to see if there were any chemical residues on it. But he never found any evidence of stolen material in the straw.

Many years later, after the Soviet Union fell, the former guard happened to see the worker in a local bar. The man looked prosperous, so the guard came up and introduced himself. "After all these years, now that I'm no longer in any position of authority, I just have to know: what were you stealing on that construction project? I'll buy you a vodka if you'll just tell me." The workman leaned in close, winked, and whispered, "Wheelbarrows."

Your problems won't always be obvious, but they might be easier to spot if you are vigilant. A surprising number of the things that can take down a startup are hiding in plain sight, but the entrepreneur has to be willing to confront uncomfortable clues. A successful entrepreneur can always use a healthy dose of skepticism, an alert mind, and a sharp eye.

W IS FOR WORK ETHIC

The first entrepreneur was probably a farmer. He and his hunter-gatherer buddies had spent a long day tracking and spearing a wooly mammoth, and they were spending the evening roasting its haunches by the fire and painting the story of their hunt on the cave walls. He looked around at his clan, rubbing mud in their wounds and wishing they had a more balanced diet—perhaps a nice salad or pie to go with their roast mammoth. He thought, "I want to start something new and different, where I could stay in one place, grow things, and sell to the neighboring clans." Long before there were hipsters in co-working lofts designing time-wasting social media apps, there were farmers.

First-generation farmers who clear the trees and rocks to carve a business out of the wilderness have always understood the realities of entrepreneurship. They mark out the first fields, plow the first furrows, and build the first houses and barns on the new land. They borrow money to do all that, and to buy and lay in the first seeds, because they are making a bet that they can produce a crop they can sell at a profit. Lots of them have succeeded and lots of them have failed, but you'd better believe they were entrepreneurs, the kind that are "all in" on their businesses. Every day was blood, sweat, tears, and the fear of bankruptcy.

No entrepreneurs have ever worked harder than farmers. How hard? In 1978, the iconic radio host Paul Harvey gave a speech called "So God Made a Farmer." Here are some excerpts:

> God said, "I need somebody willing to get up before dawn, milk cows, work all day in the fields, milk cows again, eat supper, and then go to town and stay past midnight at a meeting of the school board." So God made a farmer.
>
> "I need somebody with arms strong enough to rustle a calf

W
is for
WORK ETHIC

and yet gentle enough to deliver his own grandchild. Somebody to call hogs, tame cantankerous machinery, come home hungry, have to wait for lunch until his wife's done feeding visiting ladies, and tell the ladies to be sure and come back real soon—and mean it." So God made a farmer.

God said, "I need somebody willing to sit up all night with a newborn colt. And watch it die. Then dry his eyes and say, 'Maybe next year.' I need somebody who can shape an ax handle from a persimmon sprout, shoe a horse with a hunk of car tire, who can make a harness out of haywire, feed sacks and shoe scraps. And who, at planting time and harvest season, will finish his forty-hour week by Tuesday at noon, then, pain'n from 'tractor back,' put in another seventy-two hours." So God made a farmer.

God said, "I need somebody strong enough to clear trees and heave bails, yet gentle enough to tame lambs and wean pigs and tend the pink-combed pullets, who will stop his mower for an hour to splint the broken leg of a meadowlark. It had to be somebody who'd plow deep and straight and not cut corners. Somebody to seed, weed, feed, breed and rake and disc and plow and plant and tie the fleece and strain the milk and replenish the self-feeder and finish a hard week's work with a five-mile drive to church." So God made a farmer.

Let me say this as clearly as I can: if you don't have a strong work ethic, don't start a business. Every year, there are fewer folks who grew up doing farm chores as kids. Don't get me wrong, some great entrepreneurs were city kids, but they worked as hard as farm kids did. Bill Gates and Steve Jobs may have never milked a cow or had dirt under their fingernails, but they had a farmer's work ethic stamped into their souls. Entrepreneurship is just hard work. If you don't like or want to work that hard, if you don't have the character to start grinding and producing before sunrise and keep at it until you crawl into bed after your spouse and kids have been asleep for three hours, then stop now and get a job. You don't have it in you to be a real entrepreneur.

We've all heard a thousand pithy sayings about hard work,

until they've become clichés. Well, sayings usually become clichés because they're true. So, just to make sure we're on the same page, here are a smattering of quotes that pound the point home:

"Every morning in Africa, a gazelle wakes up. It knows it must run faster than the fastest lion or it will be killed. Every morning a lion wakes up. It knows it must outrun the slowest gazelle or it will starve to death. It doesn't matter whether you are a lion or a gazelle: when the sun comes up, you'd better be running."
—Unknown

"Without labor nothing prospers." *—Sophocles*

"Success is dependent upon the glands—sweat glands."
—Zig Ziglar

"Let us rather run the risk of wearing out than rusting out."
—Theodore Roosevelt

"The fight is won or lost far away from witnesses—behind the lines, in the gym, and out there on the road, long before I dance under those lights." *—Muhammad Ali*

"If people knew how hard I had to work to gain my mastery, it would not seem so wonderful at all." *—Michelangelo*

"Every time you stay out late, every time you sleep in, every time you miss a workout, every time you don't give one hundred per cent—you make it that much easier for me to beat you."
—Unknown

The biblical book of Proverbs has dozens of references to the lazy person with no work ethic, who it calls "the sluggard." Here's just one (Proverbs 6:6-11):

"Go to the ant, you sluggard;
  consider its ways and be wise!
It has no commander,

no overseer or ruler,
yet it stores its provisions in summer
and gathers its food at harvest.
How long will you lie there, you sluggard?
When will you get up from your sleep?
A little sleep, a little slumber,
a little folding of the hands to rest—
and poverty will come on you like a thief
and scarcity like an armed man."

That's what waits for the sluggard, for the entrepreneur with no work ethic: poverty.

In philosophical terms, a work ethic is a "necessary but not sufficient" condition for entrepreneurial survival, much less success. A work ethic doesn't guarantee success, but the lack of one pretty much guarantees failure. If you don't have one, don't try to start a business. Period. Full stop.

Calling it a work *ethic* implies that there is an ethical or moral dimension to work. This is a remnant of the Judeo-Christian worldview, the notion that purposeful productivity is a virtue, part of the image of God in Adam and Eve, before they bit the apple. Sloth makes the list as one of Christianity's Seven Deadly Sins. The Bible drives this point home over and over, including St. Paul's admonition that "the one who is unwilling to work shall not eat" (2 Thessalonians 3:10).

Our culture has lost any sense of a work *ethic*. Work ought to be considered a privilege, but our culture hates it. We see it as an affliction that must be endured to get what we *really* want: money, prestige, power, and—most importantly and ironically—the right *not* to work anymore, or to work less. Our goal is to get as much money and recognition as possible for as little effort as possible, so it will be possible to do less work in the future.

We undermine a cultural work ethic with the notion that work is unethical. Large swaths of our culture demand and have created an entitlement society in which work is seen as a necessary evil at best and cruel oppression at worst. In previous generations, and still in some circles, entrepreneurs were heroes for creating new jobs, wealth, and opportunities for others. They were role models of diligent effort. In the entitlement society, entrepreneurs are the villains—not job creators, but enslavers of entitled souls to cruel drudgery for the bread they deserve anyway.

Increasingly, I meet wannabe entrepreneurs with no work ethic, spoiled by the entitlement society (they assume they are entitled by the universe to succeed in their business) or poisoned by the cults and scams around get-rich-quick celebrity entrepreneurs. These gurus convince lazy and gullible folks who don't have enough of a work ethic to maintain even a regular job that they can take a shortcut to success by starting a business. In these deluded schemes, entrepreneurship consists of nothing but marketing, networking, and a tricky business model that all the successful people supposedly know but keep secret to hold back average folks. Listen to *me,* not to these gurus: interview a hundred entrepreneurs who started genuinely successful and sustainable businesses and ninety-nine of them will tell you that their journey was no shortcut, but a hard road full of long days bracketed by early mornings and late nights.

But still, I meet wannabe and poseur entrepreneurs who think they're supposed to be in the coolest new pub by three o'clock, laughing it up with their clever and successful friends. More than 2,000 years ago, Proverbs 21:25 noted, "The craving of a sluggard will be the death of him, because his hands refuse to work." The irony is that the sluggard is a fool who rejects being called a sluggard. He thinks he's found the secret to success, and only drudges are stupid enough to labor. To which Proverbs 26:16 replies, "A sluggard is wiser in his own eyes than seven people who answer discreetly."

It's time to tell yourself the truth. If you've started a business and it isn't succeeding as soon or as much as you had hoped, you owe it to yourself and the people who depend on you to examine your work ethic. If you're thinking about starting a business, take a pause and a deep look into your own heart. Just how hard do you want to work? How hard are you willing to work? How hard have you worked in the past? Not just in an occasional big push, but in a sustained way, as a lifestyle? As a dimension or demonstration or extension of your character? Do you have a work ethic, or are you always going to be looking for a way to do as little as possible to get the prize? You don't owe me an answer. You owe it to yourself.

X is for XENOMORPHIC

X IS FOR XENOMORPHIC

Anyone who writes an alphabet book reaches this crisis: what starts with X? Are entrepreneurs *xanthic* (yellow or yellowish)? *Xerophilous* (capable of thriving in a hot, dry climate)? *Xylopha-gous* (eating, boring into, or destroying wood)?

After considering the other qualities in this book, I'm going with *xenomorphic*. The root *xeno-* means foreign (*xenophobia* is the fear of foreigners), and *-morphic* means the form something takes (*anthropomorphic* is something that takes human form). Xe-nomorphic means having an unusual, strange, foreign shape.

How does that apply to entrepreneurs? Well, the word is used almost exclusively in the science of petrography, the classification of different types of rocks. A xenomorph, or xenomorphic rock, is a crystal that has taken on an unusual form because the sur-rounding non-crystalline rocks have impressed their form upon it. Its environment has shaped, warped, or pressured it until it has become something surprising and unique.

Look at the other twenty-five qualities in this book and con-sider just how xenomorphic entrepreneurs really are. They are unusual people. They aren't superheroes. In fact, we need to stop thinking of them as heroes at all, much less practically worship-ping them as the "cult of the entrepreneur" in startup culture con-stantly encourages. But like superheroes in comics and movies, entrepreneurs have strange qualities that can make them seem odd, even weird, to those around them. Those qualities *are* supe-rior powers—but only in the realm of starting businesses, not in the rest of life. Successful entrepreneurs might be immoral, lousy husbands or wives, terrible mothers or fathers, unreliable friends, unlikeable as people, and unable to carry a tune, sew a button, or housebreak a puppy. But by definition they have successfully started a business. That makes them unusual, and it means that they have superior abilities in that venue of life.

Are all the other qualities described in this book products of nature or nurture? Superman is super because he's from the planet Krypton and the yellow sun of Earth confers godlike powers on him. Spiderman is an ordinary (albeit nerdy) kid who got bit by a radioactive spider and found he could climb walls. Batman is an ordinary mortal who gave himself powers through technology and training. Are successful entrepreneurs born with the ability to start a business? Did some unusual event in their life transform them? Are they self-made, teaching themselves how to do it while acquiring the right set of tools?

I think successful entrepreneurs are most like the X-Men, which works out, given that this is the X chapter. In the comics and the movies, the X-Men are mutants, people with quirky or bizarre traits in their DNA. Early in life they realized they were different, but weren't always sure how or why or what to do with these qualities. In some cases they hid them and tried to act normal, to fit in. Others were ostracized, never finding their niches in life. But somewhere along the way, they became aware of and embraced their abilities and learned to channel them to some constructive purpose. Some of them use their powers to help humanity, others to hurt it. They are misunderstood and mistrusted. They are products of both nature and nurture, of the interaction between their DNA and their environment—and their own choices. They aren't like the world around them, but they have been shaped and formed by it.

I suppose that's true of everyone, but for our purposes it's an important point to remember about entrepreneurs. There's an old saying among sports coaches: you can't put in what God left out. Reading through the rest of this book ought to encourage some and sober others. Not everyone is born with the ability to successfully start a business. Those who aren't might try, and a few might even succeed in spite of their lack of talent, but they're square pegs in round holes. It will always feel like hard work to them, against the grain, uphill into the wind. Doing what you're not designed to do is a hard way to make a living and a tough way to get through a career. On the other hand, some people find that starting businesses comes naturally to them, just like some folks have a natural facility for languages, music, or sports. Some people develop skills easily as an extension of their natural talents. Would-be entrepreneurs ought to honestly appraise themselves in light of the qualities identified in this book and ask themselves, "Is this me? Could this be me?"

On the other hand, no one should think that entrepreneurship is a talent. Sure, some people are born with a capacity to incarnate the other twenty-five qualities in this book, but unless those are developed, they're just potential. Potential can be paralyzing. Most people who have been successful at anything got there by making incremental progress, focusing on what was achievable, succeeding and moving on to the next challenge. Someone who thinks they have natural entrepreneurial talent might never succeed because they either take it for granted that someday they'll get around to doing it and don't develop that gift, or they crash and burn in a series of overreaches and under-performances.

So, are successful entrepreneurs born or made? Yes. They are peculiar people with very particular abilities shaped by their DNA, parents, upbringing, education, early work experiences, the demands of life, etc. Like a rock that is unlike the rocks around it but shaped by the surrounding strata, they stand out. They aren't more beautiful or valuable, but they are unique. They have a look about them, a demeanor, and a manner of speaking and interacting with their environment. To be fair, we can recognize other professions: at a party, you can probably tell the fighter pilot from the kindergarten teacher or the rodeo cowboy from the insurance salesman. Although successful entrepreneurs come in every shape, size, color, and gender, there is something indefinable but recognizable about them. Do you see it in yourself? If so, work to cultivate and develop it, because you'll never be working in alignment with your nature until you do. But if, as you read this book, you realize in your heart of hearts that you aren't this sort of X-Man or X-Woman, then carefully consider whether starting a business is really for you.

Y is for
YEARNING

Y IS FOR YEARNING

The story behind an iconic 1980s pop song is a tale of yearning, of insatiable hunger.

The third installment of the *Rocky* movie franchise was released in 1982. In *Rocky III*, Rocky (Sylvester Stallone) is rich and famous. The heavyweight champion of the world has defended his title ten times. His family lives in a mansion and he drives a Ferrari. He's all over television, his face is on products, and there's a bronze statue of him at the top of the stairs leading up to the Philadelphia Museum of Art, where he famously trained as an unknown fighter.

But there's a new challenger coming after him. Clubber Lang (Mr. T) is lean, mean, and dangerous. He wants what Rocky has, and is willing to pay any price to take the title for himself. He challenges Rocky's pride, gets his shot, and absolutely beats the snot out of Rocky in the ring. Rocky had never fought anyone that intense, that hungry, who came after him with such fury and desire.

Afterward, Rocky tries to pick up the pieces and make sense of how he lost the title. His old opponent, Apollo Creed (Carl Weathers), offers to train Rocky for a rematch. Rocky is reluctant after the beating he took and his wife wonders what would be different the second time around. Creed takes Rocky out of the suburbs, back to an inner-city gym to train with the poor club fighters who make a few dollars per match. That's what Rocky was once, but success has spoiled and softened him. In a dramatic scene, Creed walks Rocky through the gym and tells him to look at the young men working so hard in such Spartan surroundings. The young boxers stop training and glare hungrily at the famous former champion.

"You see that look in their eyes, Rock?" asks Creed. "When we first fought I trained hard, but I didn't have that look in my eyes.

You had it, and you won." The young boxers are murmuring, like animals getting ready to attack. "Gotta get that look back, Rock. Eye of the tiger, man, eye of the tiger."

During the inevitable training montage, the motivational soundtrack is a song created for the film by the band Survivor. It became a monster hit during the 80s, and has been on many a workout playlist since. The lyrics are practically an anthem for the true entrepreneurial personality:

> *Risin' up, back on the street*
> *Did my time, took my chances*
> *Went the distance now I'm back on my feet*
> *Just a man and his will to survive*
>
> *So many times it happens too fast*
> *You trade your passion for glory*
> *Don't lose your grip on the dreams of the past*
> *You must fight just to keep them alive*
>
> *It's the eye of the tiger, it's the thrill of the fight*
> *Risin' up to the challenge of our rivals*
> *And as the last known survivor stalks his prey in the night*
> *And he's watchin' us all with the eye of the tiger*
>
> *Face to face, out in the heat*
> *Hangin' tough, stayin' hungry*
> *They stack the odds, still we take to the street*
> *For the kill with the skill to survive*
> *The eye of the tiger*
> *The eye of the tiger*

Anyone who has started a business knows moments of discouragement, despondency, depression—even despair. Anyone considering starting a business needs to go into it expecting those moments. When they come, *and they will,* the entrepreneur's desire must be stronger than his or her despair. Entrepreneurs must have a fire in their belly, a vision of what they want to do that burns so bright it cuts through the darkness of those moments when failure seems final and fatal, when losing threatens to get the last word on their careers. At those times, they have to really want it badly enough, to intensely yearn to win, to crave success in their bones and ache to achieve. They had better have the eye of the tiger, otherwise they will get beaten: by bad bets on products or people, by competitors who were smarter or luckier or hungrier, by all the things they should have seen coming and the things they didn't know they didn't know. This is a tough game with high stakes. Entrepreneurs who succeed will tell you that there were days when nothing but their will to survive kept them on their feet, when they had to fight just to get up and make one more payroll so they would have a chance to pull it out of the fire. But those who came through the fire will also get a little emotional, remembering the thrill of the fight and how they rose to the challenge of their rivals. It was kill or be killed, and they came out on top. Half-hearted doesn't cut it in entrepreneurship. Entrepreneurs have to yearn for it. The dictionary defines yearning as a feeling of intense longing for something. It is a craving, a desire, a hunger or thirst, an aching lust. Eye of the tiger, man, eye of the tiger.

I meet a lot of wannabe entrepreneurs and poseurs who don't yearn to start a successful business—they just want the rewards that success brings. Ultimately, real entrepreneurs don't yearn for the money—yes, that's the scorecard to measure performance, and they have a burning need to win—but they *love the fight.* Real entrepreneurs need to start businesses and launch products like fish need to swim and birds need to fly. It's in their nature. In the movie, Apollo Creed teaches Rocky that the true fighter yearns to win the fight because it's an extension of his life force. Wannabes and poseurs want money and recognition and all the pleasures that success can bring, and they see starting and launching a business as a necessarily evil to get them to the good life. They work only as hard as they have to, and no harder, to get what they want. If they could jump over all the starting and launching and hard work, they would. But true entrepreneurs will keep fighting, competing, inventing, launching, and starting until the day they die.

You can see it in the eyes of entrepreneurs who are the real deal. They may be the nicest neighbors, the most gentle family members, and the most devout believers. But in the ring, in the world of starting successful businesses, these are hard men and women. They are alpha predators, the top of the food chain in their market. They will win or die trying. The wannabes and poseurs? They're just looking for a shortcut to success, stupidly believing that entrepreneurship is a scheme that, if pulled off, will lead to easy money for little work. You can see it in their eyes: they're the hunted, not the hunter.

You want to start a business? Look in the mirror. What do you see? Eye of the tiger?

Z IS FOR ZEALOUS

I'll admit it: I learned to appreciate the culinary arts by watching *Iron Chef*. In fact, *Iron Chef* was the gateway drug to my becoming a more hardcore foodie.

In case you don't know, *Iron Chef* was a Japanese television show that was adapted for American television on the Food Network. It's got kind of a cheesy premise, in which a challenger chef enters "Kitchen Stadium" and calls out one of a pantheon of culinary superheroes, the Iron Chefs, to a one-hour competition. A campy master of ceremonies, the Chairman of Kitchen Stadium, unveils a secret ingredient ("Salmon!"), and the Iron Chef and the challenger have exactly one hour to produce a five-course gourmet meal for a panel of expert judges.

When I began to watch *Iron Chef*, most of the dishes produced seemed too esoteric for my tastes. But over time, I began to understand this art form. It's a unique art in that it's consumable and temporary. But I realized the passion, imagination, and mastery that these great chefs brought to their craft was at least as great as more traditional arts like writing, music, painting, etc.

That led me to appreciate other food artists: brewmasters, vintners, and restaurateurs. And the more I learned about the foodie world, the more I began to recognize that these folks weren't just passionate artists—many of them were master-class entrepreneurs as well. It's hard to imagine a more difficult business to launch than a successful, independently-owned restaurant. A chef-owner has to possess the full range of entrepreneurial gifts. He or she must be qualified in the craft. The chef-owner has to manufacture an original product in a crowded and competitive marketplace, price it correctly to produce a profit, market and sell, manage the supply chain, hire and fire, develop and oversee facilities, serve customers, endlessly deal with finances, negotiate

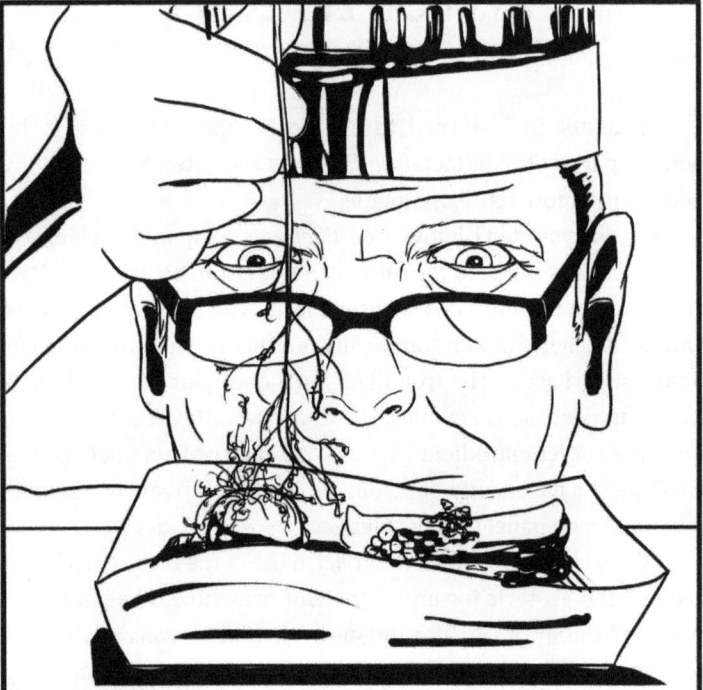

Z is for
ZEALOUS

with vendors, and pass government inspections. The margins are tight, the hours are long, and the risk is breathtaking.

But the more I learn about the great chefs who become great restaurateurs, the more I respect them for their zealous devotion to food. I'm not talking about mediocre restaurant owners who are just trying to make a buck—although as I've said over and over in this book, there's nothing wrong with trying to make a buck. The great chefs are definitely trying to make lots of bucks. But they're not *just* trying to do that. They believe in their art and are passionate about creating truly great food, as much as the authors, musicians, and filmmakers I know are zealous about making a living creating sublime examples of their crafts. As someone who writes for a living, I can honestly say that earning two Michelin Stars or becoming an Iron Chef is far harder and is a greater measure of entrepreneurial accomplishment than having a best-selling song or novel.

Zeal is defined as "fervor for a person, cause, or object; eager desire or endeavor, enthusiastic diligence; ardor." It's not just passion. Passion is fervor, but not necessarily in action. I'm passionate for great food, wine, and beer, but not zealous for it. Zealous would mean that I had applied diligence and ardor to the art (just eating it doesn't count). The opposite of zeal is to make an apathetic, lackadaisical, mediocre effort.

So, our final essential quality for the successful entrepreneur is zeal for what he or she does. Entrepreneurs that are apathetic, lackadaisical, or mediocre toward their craft had better become zealous fast, or they won't be entrepreneurs for long.

Pearl Buck wrote *The Good Earth*, which won the 1932 Pulitzer Prize for Literature. It's a finely-crafted novel that tells the story of a Chinese farmer's zeal for his land. Buck said that the key to enjoying one's career is to become zealous for doing something great. "The secret of joy in work," she said, "is contained in one word: excellence. To know how to do something well is to enjoy it."

Thomas Aquinas, the greatest of the medieval thinkers, said that, "The test of the artist does not lie in the will with which he goes to work, but in the excellence of the work he produces." In other words, great results matter more than great passion. You can't just be passionate about passion. That's like being in love with being in love, or being zealous for zeal. There has to be a point, an end, a product. When you're zealous for *that* thing to be great, and when you devote your career to making it so, then you've aligned your internal and external selves, and energy hums through your life.

One way to become more zealous for your work is to taste success. Winning breeds more wins. Losing is discouraging; when you come up short and miss goals, the zeal drains out of you. They say that you learn more from losing than winning. Maybe, sometimes. But if you're not careful, you only learn how to lose. Some people become comfortable with losing and come to accept it as normal. Their sense of self-worth may go down, but not always. They just become convinced that victory is a low-percentage phenomenon and become content with mediocre performance (at least that's how I've come to look at my golf game). If we aren't careful, losing becomes a disease. Loss breeds loss, until we become numb to failure. We don't evaluate afterwards, we don't learn or grow, and we don't try harder next time. We just shrug and accept our lot. For losing to have value, we must undertake the effort to understand why we lost. If that post-mortem examination leads us to reevaluate our abilities and our pride in them, then it can be a humbling but constructive experience. If we then use that to improve ourselves or our odds for success next time, then losing might be very instructive. The best thing we can do is recalibrate, find a way to win, and allow our zeal for what we do to build on itself.

Earlier in this book, I said that no one pays you for passion. That's true. But if your passion drives you to produce something excellent, then you start winning. People will pay you to produce excellent products, services, art, or meals. So, passion for the product and the process of making it is a critical ingredient for the entrepreneur. You have to care. If you don't, get out now.

You owe it to yourself to care, to be zealous for what you do. By self-discipline, skill, and the promise of reward, you might be able to drive yourself to do things that you don't really care about—but that's a hard way to live. Starting a business is just too damned difficult to spend your life doing something that leaves you lukewarm.

There is a peril to passion: it might lead you to things you care about but have no talent for. For example, I'm passionate about brilliant chefs, but I have no talent for cooking and would be a disastrous restaurateur. But there is also a promise to passion: in the darkest hours of your entrepreneurial career (of which there will be plenty), you will at least be doing something that matters to *you*. And in the best hours, your brightest moments of success, you'll say to yourself, "I can't believe I get paid to do this. Don't tell my customers, but I'd do it for free!"

Aligning your profession with your passion by no means guarantees you success (you might not be good at what you love), but it does make the effort easier to accept or even enjoy. So, if you're going to become an entrepreneur, if you're going to start a business, start one that you can be zealous for.

* 9 7 8 0 9 9 1 3 0 9 5 0 4 *